THE NEW YORK YANKEES

MATT CHRISTOPHER

The #1 Sports Series for Kids

★ LEGENDARY SPORTS TEAMS ★

THE NEW YORK YANKEES

Text by Glenn Stout

LITTLE, BROWN AND COMPANY

New York · Boston

Little, Brown and Company

Hachette Book Group USA
237 Park Avenue, New York, NY 10017
Visit our Web site at www.lb-kids.com

www.mattchristopher.com

First Edition: March 2008

Matt Christopher® is a registered trademark of
Matt Christopher Royalties, Inc.

Text written by Glenn Stout

Library of Congress Cataloging-in-Publication Data

Christopher, Matt.
    The New York Yankees / Matt Christopher. — 1st ed.
        p. cm. — (Legendary sports teams)
    ISBN-13: 978-0-316-01115-0 (pbk.)
    ISBN-10: 0-316-01115-0 (pbk.)
    1. New York Yankees (Baseball team) — Juvenile literature.   I. Title.
    GV875.N4C57   2007
    796.357'64097471 — dc22

                                                    2007012330

10 9 8 7 6 5 4 3 2 1

COM-MO

Printed in the United States of America

Contents

★ CHAPTER ONE ★
1903–1919

A Team for New York

The New York Yankees are the most successful franchise in the history of American professional sports. Since the team was created in 1903, the Yankees have been American League champions 39 times and won the World Series 26 times. No other team in any sport has won so many championships. That record is even more remarkable in light of the fact that in the first 18 years of their existence, the Yankees not only didn't win a World Series title, they didn't even win a pennant. In fact, they were one of the worst teams in baseball!

In 1903 there were two major leagues: the long-established National League, which was founded in 1874, and the upstart American League, which was created in 1901. After competing against each other in 1901 and 1902, the two leagues formally agreed to work together in 1903. As part of that agreement, the National League agreed to allow the American League to put a team in New York.

In early January 1903, Ban Johnson, the president of the American League, decided to move a flagging team from Baltimore to New York. There was only one problem with his plan: the team had no place to play. There were two ballparks in New York City, but both were the home fields of the National League teams. So Johnson needed to build a new park. But where, and how?

The solution didn't come easily. At the time, the government of New York City was controlled by a group of corrupt politicians known as Tammany Hall after the building where they often met. Every time Johnson thought he had found a place to build a ballpark, the politicians found a way to block him. Johnson finally realized that if he sold the team to a member of Tammany Hall, he would be allowed to build a ballpark.

That's exactly what happened. Johnson agreed to sell the team to two members of Tammany Hall, Frank Farrell, a gambler, and William Devery, the former chief of police of New York City. Soon after, he received permission to build a ballpark in the northern part of Manhattan.

With that issue resolved, Johnson set out to build his team. He had promised Devery and Farrell that the team would be a winner, so he needed quality players and leadership. He got them by cherry-picking other teams.

Clark Griffith, a former pitcher and manager of the 1901 American League champion Chicago White Stockings, became manager of the new team. Star pitcher Jack Chesbro of the Pittsburgh Pirates and outfielder Dave Fultz of the Philadelphia Athletics both made the move to New York, but the big star was outfielder "Wee Willie" Keeler, who left the Brooklyn Dodgers for the new Manhattan team. Although Keeler wasn't a big man or a slugger, he knew how to hit; he once famously described his approach by saying that he "hit 'em where they ain't."

The new team played its first game on April 22 in Washington, D.C., against the Senators, losing, 3–1. Eight days later, on April 30, they won their first home game, 6–2, in their new park. The stands in American League Park — the official name of the place most knew as Hilltop Park, due to its location on one of the highest points on the island of Manhattan — were not quite finished, and parts of the field didn't have any grass. But no one watching the game seemed to mind. They were just enjoying the action.

As of yet the team didn't have an official name. Most fans just called them the Americans, to distinguish the club from New York's National League team, the Giants. But within a year some fans and newspaper reporters were referring to the new team as the Highlanders, while others called them the Hilltoppers. Still others called them the Yankees because they played in the northern part of Manhattan and the term "Yankee" referred to Americans who lived in the northeast. This last name stuck and in 1913, it became official.

Over the course of their first season, the Yankees picked up several more talented players, such as fiery shortstop Kid Elberfeld. By midseason, they were in the pennant race. Then they fell back, finishing in fourth place with a record of 72–62, 17 games behind pennant-winning Boston.

In the off-season, Johnson arranged for a few trades to make the Yankees stronger. On opening day in 1904 New York beat Boston, 8–2, sending the message that the Yankees were just as good as the champions.

The Yankees were particularly successful when Jack Chesbro was on the mound. Chesbro was one of the first pitchers to throw the spitball, a pitch that was legal at the time but has since been banned. Chesbro spit on his fingers then squeezed the ball out like a watermelon seed as he threw it. That wet squeeze made the ball quickly dart toward the ground just as it reached home plate. The pitch was so effective, and Chesbro so strong, that other American League teams usually lost when he pitched.

By season's end, however, Boston held first place, with a record of 92–57 to the Yankees' 90–56. The two teams were scheduled to play each other five times. The winner of the series would take home the pennant.

The Yankees won the first game, but Boston won the next two. On the last day of the season, October 10, the two teams were scheduled to play a doubleheader. To win the pennant, the Yankees needed to win both games.

Jack Chesbro started the game for New York. Three days earlier, he had beaten Boston for his 41st victory of the season, a modern-day record. The next day he pitched again but lost. Now he was pitching for the third time in four days.

An overflow crowd of 30,000 fans packed every nook and cranny of Hilltop Park that afternoon. In the fifth inning the Yankees squeezed two runs across the plate to take a 2–0 lead. Then, in the seventh inning, Boston scored two runs to tie it up. The score remained 2–2 to the top of the ninth. Chesbro and the Yankees needed to hold Boston scoreless while adding a run of their own to win the game.

Boston's first batter, Lou Criger, hit a ground ball to shortstop. Elberfeld fielded it cleanly, but threw the ball into the dirt in front of first. Criger was safe. Then Boston pitcher Bill Dinneen bunted him to second base. The next at bat, Criger went to third base on a ground ball out.

Now Boston shortstop Fred Parent stepped up to the plate. Chesbro was exhausted, but he knew he needed to get at least one more out. He worked the count to one ball, two strikes. Everyone knew he was going to throw a spitball next. That was his best pitch and almost the only pitch he ever threw. In fact, he had already struck out Parent twice on spitballs.

This time, something went wrong. Instead of the ball darting across the plate for strike three, the ball squirted from Chesbro's hand and sailed over Fred Parent's head. Chesbro's catcher Red Kleinow leaped for the pitch, but it was too high. As the ball rattled against the backstop, Criger scrambled home. Boston led, 3–2!

Chesbro was stunned. He gave up a single and then finally got the third out of the inning. He walked off the field and collapsed on the bench in tears. Yankee manager Clark Griffith was crushed. He fell to the ground and buried his face in the dust.

The Yankees tried to rally in the bottom of the inning but fell short. Boston won the game, and the pennant, on Chesbro's wild pitch. The pitcher later told a reporter, "I would have given my entire salary back could I but had the ball back."

Despite the loss, most baseball fans expected the Yankees to contend for the pennant for the next year. But in 1905 many of their key pitchers were injured, including Jack Chesbro, and the Yankees finished in sixth place.

The highlight of the season was the play of rookie first baseman Hal Chase. Before Chase joined the Yankees, most first basemen played only a few steps off the bag. They rarely pursued ground balls.

Chase revolutionized the position. He ranged far off the base yet still managed to make it back in time to receive a throw. If he saw a batter start to bunt, Chase charged the hitter, sometimes fielding the ball on the third-base side of the diamond. He was wildly popular with Yankee fans, who called him Prince Hal.

Still the Yankees fell short in 1905; and although they rallied in 1906, finishing three games out of first place, they didn't do much for the following ten years. Corruption began to seep into the ranks, with the worst case being the discovery that Hal Chase had been "fixing" games — betting against his team and then playing poorly so they'd lose. Owners Frank Farrell and William Devery squandered any money the team made on themselves instead of using it to build a stronger squad. The ballpark itself began to fall apart and in 1914 was in such a state of disrepair that the Yankees had to rent the Polo Grounds from the Giants to play their home games.

In short, the Yankees were the laughingstock of the American League. With the team losing money year after year, Farrell and Devery decided to get out of the game. At the end of the 1914 season, they put the Yankees up for sale.

Jacob Ruppert, the wealthy owner of a New York brewery, was a big baseball fan. So was Colonel Tillinghast L'Hommedieu "Cap" Huston, an engineer who had served in the Spanish American War. Ruppert and Cap Huston were friends, and when they heard that the Yankees were available, they made Devery and Farrell an offer. Devery and Farrell accepted — and a new chapter in the history of the New York Yankees began.

★ CHAPTER TWO ★

1920–1928

Enter the Babe

Ruppert and Huston bought the Yankees knowing they would have to rebuild the crumbling franchise. They were prepared to spend whatever it cost to get new players and make the Yankees contenders for the pennant. They also knew they would soon need their own ballpark, one that rivaled the new stadiums recently built by the Giants and the Dodgers.

Ruppert and Huston went after the players first. In 1915 they purchased pitcher Bob Shawkey from the Athletics for $15,000. In 1916 they talked former A's third baseman Frank "Home Run" Baker out of retirement and paid the A's $25,000 to allow Baker to sign a contract with the Yankees. With these two starters, and star first baseman Wally Pipp, the 1916 Yankees won more games than they lost for the first time since 1910. Attendance at Yankee games, low for many years, suddenly doubled.

Huston and Ruppert didn't rest, however. They continued to acquire better players through smart trades and outright contract purchases. They also hired Miller Huggins, a former infielder, to manage the team. Their aggressive strategy paid off in 1919, when the Yankees ended the year only seven and a half games behind the champion Chicago White Sox.

That same season, Ruppert and Huston took notice of one particular player from Boston. The burly, moon-faced man was said to be undisciplined, but he had loads of talent. He had started his career as a pitcher for the Red Sox, but in 1918, due to a shortage of players because of World War I, he began playing in the outfield and taking a regular turn at the plate. His name was George Herman Ruth, but everyone called him Babe.

Until Babe Ruth came along, home runs were rare. Batters didn't swing hard — they just tried to make contact with the ball. Ruth was different. He swung from his heels and hit the ball a long way. In 1919, he was on his way to hitting more homers than any other player in Major League Baseball's history.

Yet for all his talent, Ruth was also one of the most aggravating players in baseball. He argued with umpires, ran around at all hours of the night, and sometimes didn't bother to show up for games. He had been suspended from the Red Sox many times and always promised to shape up, but his behavior never improved for very long.

Red Sox owner Harry Frazee was getting impatient with his slugger. In 1919, the Red Sox were desperate for good pitching. But Ruth refused to pitch. That made Frazee angry. Then Ruth threatened to retire at the end of the season — despite being under contract for 1920 — unless Frazee doubled his salary!

That was it for Harry Frazee. He let it be known that Ruth was up for grabs.

Ruppert and Huston jumped at the chance to add Ruth's name to their roster. They had seen how Yankee fans cheered him every time he came to the plate, even though he often helped the Red Sox beat their team. Confident that Ruth would fill the stands, they offered Frazee $125,000 for the slugger. It was the largest purchase price in baseball history at the time, a price that Frazee readily accepted.

Babe Ruth was now a New York Yankee.

Many people thought the Yankees were taking a big chance. They believed Ruth's record number of home runs in 1919 was a fluke. Others believed that Ruth would be even more easily distracted from the game in New York than he had been in Boston.

They needn't have worried. After a slow start Ruth hit his first home run as a Yankee on May 1, 1920, against Boston. The blast was one of the longest ever hit at the Polo Grounds, sailing over the roof of the grandstand in right field.

All summer long Ruth kept hitting home runs — and Yankee fans kept pouring into the ballpark to watch him, much to Ruppert and Huston's delight. Although the Yankees didn't win the pennant, they finished the season in third place with a record of 95–59. Ruth led the majors with 54 home runs, and the Yankees attracted more than one million fans, the first team ever to draw so many spectators. The Yankees were suddenly one of the most profitable teams in baseball.

By now, Ruppert and Huston were tired of renting

the Polo Grounds. They decided to build their own ballpark. Ruppert acquired land in the Bronx and began making plans to build the biggest baseball stadium in the world.

In the meantime, the Yankees tried to win a pennant. In 1921 Ruth proved that his 54 home runs were no fluke as he cracked 59 to lead the majors once again. The Yankees stormed to the pennant and earned the right to play the National League champions, the New York Giants, in the World Series.

Unfortunately, in the second game of the Series Ruth hurt his elbow. He could hardly lift a bat after that, and by the end of the Series he couldn't even play. The Giants won the Series five games to three, and the Yankees started looking forward to the next year.

Unfortunately for Yankee fans, 1922 ended the same way 1921 had, with the Giants besting their crosstown rivals in the World Series.

The following year, the Yankees moved into their new, state-of-the-art ballpark. Yankee Stadium boasted an enormous double-decked grandstand topped by a decorative façade, which surrounded the infield and stretched down each foul line. The outfield was huge; in fact, the fence in left center, the deepest part of the ballpark, was nearly 500 feet from home plate.

One sportswriter dubbed the Stadium "the House that Ruth Built," meaning that Ruth's popularity and prowess had made the Yankees successful enough to build such a park. But in reality, the park was built to suit Ruth. Down the right-field line, where Ruth hit many of his home runs, the fence was only 295 feet away.

On April 18, 1923, the gates of Yankee Stadium were opened for the first time. More than 60,000 fans poured in for the game, filling the stands to capacity and forcing close to 15,000 more fans to remain outside. Most of those spectators came to see Babe Ruth in action.

Ruth did not disappoint. In the fourth inning, amidst thunderous applause and cheers, he came up to bat with two runners on base. The pitcher threw. Ruth swung.

Boom!

A sound like a firecracker echoed through the park as Ruth connected with the ball. It soared high and far to right field, landing ten rows back into the stands. Babe Ruth had hit the first home run at Yankee Stadium!

From that moment on, the Yankees never looked back. They romped to first place 16 games ahead of the second-best team. With the pennant in their pockets, they headed to the World Series to face the Giants yet again. They'd lost that contest twice in a row. But this time, they blew past their rivals and took the Series in six games. Ruth helped by adding three home runs in those games.

After the victory Jacob Ruppert said, "This is the happiest day of my life. Now I have the greatest ballpark *and* the greatest team."

Unfortunately, the Yankees didn't stay at the top for long. In 1924 they finished in second place behind the Washington Senators. Then, in 1925, Ruth's hard living caught up with him.

Over the past few seasons he had spent a great deal of time partying. Always a large man, he had put on far too much weight. His health was failing, and in 1925 he collapsed during spring training. No one — then or now — was quite sure what illness Ruth had, but it was bad enough that he spent more than six weeks in the hospital. When he finally returned to the Yankees on June 1, the team was already out of the pennant race.

The lone bright spot of the season took place one day after Ruth's return — although at first it looked more like a tragedy than a boon. On June 2, Wally Pipp, the Yankee first baseman, was taking batting practice. A Yankee prospect threw an errant pitch that hit Pipp on the side of his head. At the time, batters didn't wear helmets. Pipp was badly hurt. He was rushed off the field and hurried to the hospital, where he spent the next two weeks recovering.

Back at the park, the Yankee manager needed a first baseman. He looked down the bench. His eyes settled on a quiet rookie from New York's Columbia University, Lou Gehrig. The Yankee scout who discovered him had called him "another Babe Ruth," but so far Gehrig hadn't done very much.

Nevertheless, Huggins pointed to Gehrig and said, "You're my first baseman." Gehrig grabbed his glove and ran out on the field to get ready.

From that moment on, Wally Pipp was out of a job. Gehrig lived up to his reputation and started hitting with as much power and distance as the

Babe. For the next 13 years, Gehrig played every game, earning the nickname the Iron Horse, a term used to describe a particularly powerful and dependable locomotive.

But in 1925, nothing Gehrig did made a difference. The Yankees were minus Ruth, and by the end of the season they were minus the pennant, too. But the following year, Ruth had fully recovered, and together he and Gehrig became the best one-two punch in baseball. Each hit over .300 and collected 81 extra base hits. Ruth blasted 47 home runs, and although Gehrig hit only 16, he had 20 triples.

But the Yankees had more going for them than just these two amazing players. Slugging outfielder Bob Meusel was one of the best hitters in baseball. Fleet-footed center fielder Earle Combs was a star, too, as was heavy-hitting second baseman Tony Lazzeri. The Yankee pitching staff was deep and experienced, and manager Miller Huggins was considered one of the best in the game. The Yankee roster could do it all: slug great hits, steal bases, play great defense, and outpitch the other team. They were almost unbeatable.

Almost. After winning the 1926 pennant, they

faced the St. Louis Cardinals in the World Series. The two teams split the first six games of the Series. Ruth had been magnificent, cracking four home runs. But now the world championship had come down to the final game.

And then it was down to the final inning of the final game. St. Louis held a narrow 3–2 lead, but the Yankees were up at bat. With two outs, Babe Ruth came to the plate. The Cardinal pitcher walked him. Now Bob Meusel stepped to the plate. Lou Gehrig was on deck. If Meusel and Gehrig came through, the Yankees would win.

The pitcher went into his windup. Suddenly, there was movement at first base. The crowd gasped. Babe Ruth was trying to steal second base!

That was a huge mistake. The throw beat him to second, and the Cardinals won the World Series.

Thankfully, the Yankees' performance in 1927 soon made everyone forget Ruth's foolhardy error. Simply put, the 1927 Yankees might have been the best team ever.

Almost everyone on the team had a great year. Lou Gehrig cracked 47 home runs, the most at the time by any player not named Babe Ruth. Earle

Combs hit .356 and Bob Meusel hit .337. Lazzeri, Gehrig, Meusel, and Ruth all knocked in more than 100 runs. Starting pitcher Herb Pennock won 22 games and 30-year-old Wilcy Moore earned fame as one of the first great relief pitchers in baseball.

By July 4 it was clear the Yankees would again win the American League pennant. The story now was the Ruth–Gehrig battle for the league lead in home runs. Then Ruth pulled ahead, and the question shifted from who would win the home-run race to whether the big man would meet or beat his existing record of 59 homers in a season. On September 30, he answered that question by cracking two homers to tie the record.

But he wasn't done yet. The next day, in a game against the Senators, Ruth came up in the eighth inning still looking for home run number 60. Washington pitcher Tom Zachary wasn't eager to go down in history as the man who gave him that run. He pitched carefully to the slugger.

Not carefully enough, however.

Crack! With a mighty swing, Ruth sent a wicked line drive toward right field. The ball left the park just fair and smacked into the seats. Babe Ruth had just hit his 60th home run!

Ruth was thrilled. When he had become ill in 1925, many people thought he was washed up. But that spell proved to be just the wake-up call he needed. Since that time he had changed his ways. Now he had proven that not only was he back, he was as good as he had ever been.

The Yankees faced the Pirates in the World Series. Pittsburgh was a good team, built around pitching and the hitting of the Waner brothers, Lloyd and Paul, who were known as Little Poison and Big Poison. When Babe Ruth saw them, however, he said, "They're no bigger than a couple of little kids. If I was that size I'd be afraid of getting hurt."

Nothing of any size could stop the 1927 Yankees. They steamrolled the Pirates in four straight games, making it look easy.

It was. The Yankees were so much better than everyone else that at the beginning of 1928, they won 34 of their first 42 games. A number of injuries in the second half of the season stopped them from marching over the competition completely, but they still won the pennant easily to sail to the World Series. This time, New York's opponent was the St. Louis Cardinals.

The Yankees won the first three games handily, with Lou Gehrig hitting four home runs. Babe Ruth, however, was relatively quiet.

Then in game four, Ruth woke up. He belted three home runs to help the Yankees to a 7–3 victory and their second consecutive World Series victory. The Yankees had played so well that in 36 innings of World Series baseball, St. Louis had only led for three innings. Winning the championship, it seemed, was becoming a Yankee tradition.

★ CHAPTER THREE ★

1929–1941

Building a Dynasty

No matter how good a baseball team is, it can never stay together for too long. Players age, get injured, or are traded, and new and different players have to take up the slack.

In 1929 it became clear that the Yankees were experiencing the effects of such changes. Other players and teams rose to supremacy, and by the season's final weeks it was the Philadelphia Athletics, not the New York Yankees, who were in first place.

Then the situation got even worse. In September manager Miller Huggins became ill with an infection. He died on September 23. The Yankee players were crushed, particularly Babe Ruth. Huggins had treated him like his own son.

In the end, the Yankees wound up 18 games behind

the Athletics. There would be no pennant or World Championship for the reigning champs that year.

It was time to rebuild.

The process went slowly. In both 1930 and 1931 the Yankees again finished behind Philadelphia. Ruth and Gehrig continued to play well, but New York had a difficult time replacing their other stars.

Jacob Ruppert knew that the best way to build a team was to groom young players so they'd be ready to fill the gaps when needed. The team hired a man named George Weiss to run their minor league system and develop talent.

They also took on a new manager, Joe McCarthy. Not everyone approved of McCarthy, who had managed the Chicago Cubs of the National League until he was fired in 1930. Some believed the manager's job should go to Babe Ruth — including the Babe himself.

But by midseason in 1932, McCarthy won most of them over. Under his watch, youthful pitchers Lefty Gomez and Red Ruffing both emerged as big winners and all of a sudden the Yankees were contenders once again. They romped to another pennant and, in an ironic twist, faced McCarthy's old team in the World Series.

The first two games were held in New York. The Yankees won both easily. Then the Series moved to Chicago.

Game three is one of the most famous in World Series history. It was certainly one of the most raucous, with the two dugouts trading insults and jeers from minute one. The fans were equally loud and obnoxious, particularly when Ruth came to bat.

But the big man gave as good as he got — and he backed up his taunts at the plate with a three-run homer in the first inning!

But the Cubs stormed back to tie things up 4–4 going into the fifth inning.

Then Ruth came up to bat opposite pitcher Charlie Root. The Cubs' dugout and stands let him have it, calling Ruth all sorts of names. The Babe let Root's first pitch pass by for a strike. Then he turned to the Cubs' bench and held up a finger as if saying, "That's just strike one."

After two balls Root threw another strike. Ruth didn't swing, but looked over to the Cub bench with a big grin on his face and waved his hand while holding up two fingers, as if saying, "That's just strike two."

At least that's what most people saw. Others insisted that Ruth pointed to center field, as if to say, "That's where I'm gonna hit the next pitch."

The crowd was on its feet and the Cubs were screaming, but Ruth stood calmly at the plate, waiting for the pitch. Root threw a ball over the plate.

Pow!

Ruth crushed the ball. It soared high and deep and far, over the fence, over the center-field stands, and into the street. As Ruth jogged around the bases he laughed and pointed to the Cubs. The Yankees won the game 7–5.

Ruth's home run came to be known as "the called shot," as if he had really predicted that he was going to hit the ball over the center-field fence and then did so.

Of course he really didn't, as film of the at bat clearly shows. But newspaper reporters, always eager for a good story, wrote that he had — and Ruth never denied it. After all, it had been a great shot, called or not; boosted by that classic Ruth homer, the Yankees went on to win the Series.

Ruth's fifth-inning blast was also the last great moment of his Yankee career. In 1933, he finally began showing his age. Lou Gehrig picked up some of the slack, but the Yankees fell back and failed to win the pennant that year or the next. Before the beginning of the 1935 season, the Yankees made a tough decision and released Babe Ruth. He signed with the Boston Braves but played only a few more months before retiring.

The Yankees were now Lou Gehrig's team. After being overshadowed by Ruth for most of his career, he knew it was up to him to lead New York back to first place. He would need help, however.

Fortunately, help was on the way, in the form of a young outfielder named Joe DiMaggio.

A native of San Francisco, DiMaggio first made his mark in baseball as a minor league outfielder for the San Francisco Seals of the Pacific Coast League. A great hitter, in 1933 DiMaggio amazed minor league fans by getting a hit in 61 consecutive games. He was also an excellent center fielder who appeared to glide over the ground as he ran.

DiMaggio impressed several major scouts, and a number of teams made offers to buy him. But then, in 1934, he hurt his knee. Every team but the Yankees was scared off. They paid the Seals $25,000 and gave up five players for the rights to DiMaggio. It was a big gamble but one that paid off handsomely. DiMaggio's knee healed, and he bounced back and hit almost .400 for the Seals in 1935. In 1936 the Yankees decided DiMaggio was ready to play in the majors.

From the very beginning of the season he was terrific and he just got better. By season's end he had hit .323 with 29 home runs.

The rest of the Yankees were just as strong. Many baseball historians consider the 1936 Yankees as good as — or even better than — the 1927 team. They hit .300 as a team, and five different players knocked in more than 100 runs. They won the pennant by almost 20 games and then went on to beat the Giants in the World Series.

They were nearly as good the next year, and Joe DiMaggio was even better. He smacked 46 home runs. Lou Gehrig added 37 of his own; together the duo of DiMaggio and Gehrig became almost as feared as Ruth and Gehrig had once been. The two sluggers led the Yankees to the pennant and World Series in both 1937 and 1938.

Jacob Ruppert took particular pleasure in the 1938 victory. He had been the owner of the best team in major league baseball since 1914. But now the man responsible for bringing Babe Ruth to New York and for building Yankee Stadium was dying. In mid-January of 1939, he made one final request: he wanted to see Babe Ruth one more time. Ruth rushed to his side, and Ruppert passed away a few hours later. Control of the team was transferred to general manager Ed Barrow.

Ruppert's death wasn't the only tragedy to strike the team that year. The Yankees looked forward to another championship season in 1939, but during spring training Lou Gehrig looked awful and played even worse. He couldn't hit a fastball anymore, his movements were stiff and awkward, and he sometimes stumbled or appeared as if he were losing his balance. One sportswriter described him as looking "like a man trying to lift heavy trunks into the back of a truck."

All the Yankees hoped that he would come around once the season started, but Gehrig just continued to go downhill. In eight games he only collected four hits, all weak singles.

Gehrig had never been a selfish player. He believed that he was letting the team down, so on May 2, as the Yankees prepared to play Detroit, he made a decision. He approached manager Joe McCarthy and told him, "I'm not helping the team anymore. I want you to take me out of the lineup."

McCarthy didn't argue with him. Gehrig had played in a record 2,130 consecutive games; being taken out would end that run, so McCarthy realized the Iron Horse had to be serious. Babe Dahlgren played first base as Lou Gehrig sat on the bench and watched.

Those closest to Gehrig understood then that something was very wrong with him. Gehrig himself recognized that he was sick. In June he traveled to a famous hospital in Minnesota, the Mayo Clinic, where doctors diagnosed him with a rare disease called amyotrophic lateral sclerosis (ALS).

ALS affects the body's nervous system. Over time, the nerves that control muscles stop working. Patients can no longer make their bodies do what they want them to do. Sadly, there is nothing any doctor can do to reverse the course of the disease, for there is no cure for ALS.

Lou Gehrig now knew why he was stumbling and why he couldn't hit anymore. It was because he was dying.

The baseball world was devastated when word of Gehrig's condition became public. The Yankees were particularly distraught — they weren't just going to lose a valuable player, but a good friend as well. On July 4, they decided to hold Lou Gehrig Appreciation Day at Yankee Stadium. All Gehrig's old teammates showed up, including Babe Ruth. As the Yankee crowd chanted, "We want Gehrig," Lou stepped to a microphone near home plate and gave the most famous speech in the history of baseball:

"Fans," he said, "for the past two weeks you have been reading about what a bad break I got. Yet today, I consider myself the luckiest man on the face of the earth." He went on to mention how fortunate he felt to play for the Yankees, and to have two wonderful parents and a loving wife. In closing he added, "I might have had a bad break, but I have an awful lot to live for."

Then Gehrig left the field for the last time. He died two years later, and ever since that time ALS has also been known as Lou Gehrig's disease.

, his Yankee teammates were able to fo- _ _ rest of the season. DiMaggio, in particu- _ _ s magnificent. The Yankees rolled to another pe _ nant, winning 106 games and then sweeping the Cincinnati Reds in four games to win their fourth consecutive world championship.

Yet this victory was overshadowed by terrible events that had unfolded in Europe a month earlier. On September 1, 1939, Adolf Hitler and his Nazi army invaded Poland. Two days later, Poland's allies, including England and France, had declared war on Germany. Germany's allies responded by pledging their might to Hitler's side. World War II had begun.

Many in the United States wondered if the country would join the fight against Hitler. But for the time being, President Roosevelt chose to stay out of the conflict. Still, many Americans kept an eye on the ongoing struggles overseas even as they continued with their usual activities.

One of those activities was watching baseball, and in 1940 many fans wondered if the Yankees would add a fifth World Series title to their record. They didn't. In fact, they finished in third place, behind champion Detroit and Cleveland.

The following season looked to be a repeat of the previous one, for the Yankees got off to a terrible start. On May 14 the four-time champs' record was only 14–13!

A big reason for their poor showing was because Joe DiMaggio was slumping at the plate. But one New York sportswriter noted optimistically that "when DiMaggio begins to hit again he will pull the Yankees with him."

DiMaggio got a hit the very next day. Then he got a hit in the next game. And the next game. And the *next*. By June 2 — a sad day, for Lou Gehrig passed away that day — DiMaggio's hitting streak had lengthened to 19 games. And it wasn't over, not by a long shot!

By now, fans all around the country were keeping track of DiMaggio's streak, following it as closely they were following the increasing violence in Europe.

DiMaggio did not disappoint. One way or another, he kept getting at least one hit per game. On July 2, he hit in his 45th straight game, beating the existing record of 41 set by Wee Willie Keeler in 1897.

The Yankees, meanwhile, were busy maintaining a streak of their own. From their dismal 14–13 record on May 14, they had jumped to an amazing 54–27! When DiMaggio beat Keeler's record, they were in the midst of a winning run of 14 consecutive games that began on June 28 and ended July 14.

Three days after their winning streak ended, the Yankees were set to face the Cleveland Indians at Cleveland. DiMaggio had hit in 56 straight games, an amazing feat dubbed "The Streak." He, his team, and fans everywhere were hoping he'd stretch his hits to 57 that day.

Before the game, DiMaggio shared a cab to Municipal Stadium with fellow teammate and friend Lefty Gomez. Not surprisingly, the cabdriver recognized the players, especially the one known nationwide as the Yankee Clipper. As they drove to the game, the cabbie said something to DiMaggio that has gone down in baseball history: "I gotta strange feeling in my bones that you're going to get stopped tonight."

DiMaggio, like many ballplayers, was superstitious, yet apparently he took the cabdriver's dire prediction in stride. In fact, when the cabbie dropped the players at the stadium, DiMaggio gave the man fifty cents — even though the fare itself was only twenty cents.

The game began soon after. In his first at bat, DiMaggio hit a rocket toward third baseman Ken Keltner. Some infielders might have missed the catch, but Keltner was one of the best glove men in the league. He backhanded the ball and gunned the ball to first base as DiMaggio raced toward the bag.

The ball and DiMaggio arrived almost simultaneously. But the ball got there just a second sooner. The umpire threw up his hand and yelled, "OUT!"

DiMaggio headed back to the dugout. He later blamed the muddy conditions around home plate for his slow start out of the box. But then, he didn't complain. He knew he'd have other opportunities to keep his streak alive.

But his next time up he walked. And the time after that, he grounded out to Keltner again. Suddenly, it was the eighth inning. DiMaggio had only one more chance.

With a runner on first, DiMaggio hit a hard bouncing grounder off pitcher Jim Bagby. Cleveland shortstop Lou Boudreau gloved the ball and flipped it to second. The second baseman touched the bag and then threw to first. The double play had only taken seconds, but that was plenty of time to get DiMaggio out.

The cabdriver's "strange feeling" had become a reality.

That didn't slow DiMaggio or the Yankees down. In fact, DiMaggio got hits in the next 16 games. The Yankees, meanwhile, romped to another pennant win to earn the chance to face the Brooklyn Dodgers in the World Series. The Dodgers were a great team, but they were no match for the Yankees. New York won in five games.

With that contest over, Americans turned their attention to the war in Europe. Many believed Roosevelt had kept them out of the conflict for far too long. They wondered what it would take for him to declare war.

They got their answer on December 7, 1941. That morning, the Japanese bombed Pearl Harbor. Suddenly, the United States was at war — and baseball wasn't quite as important.

☆ CHAPTER FOUR ☆

1942–1950

War Stories

Shortly after the attack on Pearl Harbor, baseball commissioner Kenesaw Mountain Landis asked President Roosevelt a question: "What do you want baseball to do?"

Roosevelt responded, "I feel it would be best for the country if baseball kept going." The President sensed that the sport known as the national pastime could help the country's morale during the war.

Like every other major-league team, the Yankees were determined to do their part. Some Yankees, like pitcher Johnny Sturm, enlisted in the military. Others joined the reserves or registered for the draft. The Yankees began the 1942 season uncertain if many of their players would be able to play the entire year.

Nevertheless, they still won 103 games and another pennant. Unfortunately, this time they lost the

World Series, falling to St. Louis in five games. A few days after the end of the Series, shortstop Phil Rizzuto joined the service. Joe DiMaggio entered a few months later. In all, a total of 26 Yankee players served in the military during World War II. Most other teams lost a similar number of players.

As Yankees traded pinstripes for fatigues, the ball club scrambled to find good players. The pickings were slim, however, with the pool consisting of those who were too young, too old, or otherwise unfit for military service. Nevertheless the team still managed to win another pennant in 1943. Outfielder Charlie Keller cracked 31 home runs, and the Yankee pitching staff was the deepest in the league. They met the Cardinals in the World Series again and beat them in five games.

The war had an even greater impact on baseball in 1944 and 1945. The Yankee roster was filled with players who otherwise may not have been in the major leagues, like second baseman Snuffy Stirnweiss, whose ulcers kept him from serving in the military. The team finished in third place in 1944 and was sold to three men, Larry MacPhail, Dan Topping, and Del

Webb. This trio couldn't build a better team, however. The Yankees finished in fourth place in 1945.

But in truth, few people but the most avid baseball followers took notice. People the world over were too busy celebrating the end of World War II, although they were just beginning to recognize the deadly impact the six-year struggle had had on the world.

Baseball was not immune to the effects of the war, of course. Players who had been at the top of their game had lost two or three years to military service. While many had stayed in shape by playing for teams sponsored by the military, they were just that much older when they returned to the game. No one knew if the players would be as good as they were before the war.

The Yankees began the 1946 season with Joe DiMaggio back in center field, but they were still missing players like Phil Rizzuto and second baseman Joe Gordon. It soon became clear that the Yankees weren't a team of stars anymore.

The Boston Red Sox, on the other hand, were loaded. Before the war, Boston was a team of promising young players, like outfielder Ted Williams and infielders Johnny Pesky and Bobby Doerr. Now all those players were in their prime. They made the Yankees look old and slow.

Boston fans were excited. Ever since Babe Ruth had been sold to the Yankees, the Red Sox had always come up short compared to New York. Now it appeared as if the two clubs were on equal footing.

Boston took command of the pennant race early in 1946. In late May, New York's manager Joe McCarthy resigned and former Yankee catcher Bill Dickey took over his position. The change didn't make any difference. The Red Sox won 104 games and the pennant. The Yankees finished third, 17 games behind.

Although the Red Sox lost the 1946 World Series to St. Louis, they were heavily favored to win the pennant in 1947. After all, they had Ted Williams, the strongest hitter in the major leagues.

The Yankees had Joe DiMaggio, of course, but prior to the start of the season, Joltin' Joe had surgery on his heel. When the season opened, he was still recovering. Over the first few weeks of the season the Yankees struggled.

Then they played the Red Sox in a four-game series. Or rather, they *crushed* the Red Sox in a four-game series, beating them, 9–0, 5–0, 17–2, and 9–3. DiMaggio completely outplayed Ted Williams, proving he still had plenty left to offer.

The victories gave the Yankees some momentum. In late June they embarked on a 19-game winning streak that put the pennant in their pockets.

Meanwhile, the Brooklyn Dodgers captured the National League pennant. They were led by rookie Jackie Robinson, the first African American to play major league baseball in the 20th century.

Robinson's presence caused many to ask when the Yankees would sign an African American player. Already, the Cleveland Indians had followed the Dodgers by making Larry Doby the first African American in the American League.

But the Yankees were slow to even consider signing African American ballplayers. The issue just wasn't important to either team president Larry MacPhail or general manager George Weiss, and the Yankees didn't feel the need to change. Eventually, their resistance to integration would prove costly.

The Yankees–Dodgers World Series was a classic thriller. In five of the first six games the two clubs fought close battles. In game four, New York pitcher Bill Bevens led, 2–1, and carried a no-hitter into the ninth inning. Brooklyn's one run had come on walks in the fifth inning. Now Bevens needed only three outs to become the first pitcher to throw a no-hitter during the World Series.

With one out he walked a batter. Then he got out Spider Jorgensen on a pop-up. Bevens was one out away from immortality. The base runner stole second, however, and then Bevens gave up yet another walk to put men at first and second.

Dodger Al Gionfriddo stepped up to the plate. Bevens pitched carefully, but Gionfriddo caught one cleanly and sliced a line drive to right field.

Yankee outfielder Tommy Henrich, knowing the no-hitter was on the line, raced back to the wall after the ball. He had two choices: go for a nearly impossible but game-ending catch, or let the ball hit the wall and then relay it as quickly as possible for the out. At the last moment he decided to go for the catch. But the ball went over his head, careening off the wall and bounding away!

As Henrich fumbled to find the ball, both Brooklyn runners dashed around the bases. Both scored.

Bevens lost his no-hitter, and the Yankees lost the ball game on one pitch.

Gionfriddo was the star in game six, too, snagging Joe DiMaggio's long drive out of the air to preserve a Brooklyn win. But in the end it didn't matter. New York came back to win game seven and their eleventh World Series title.

In 1948 the Yankees and Red Sox resumed their battle for the AL pennant. The Red Sox even hired former Yankee manager Joe McCarthy. This time, however, Boston edged out the Yankees in the final days of the season. The Red Sox finished in a tie with Cleveland, and then lost the pennant in a play-off game. The Yankees, meanwhile, fired manager Bucky Harris and hired Casey Stengel.

At first Stengel, a former player with the Brooklyn Dodgers who had failed as a manager with both Brooklyn and the Boston Braves, seemed an odd choice. He looked like a cartoon character and somehow, everything he said sounded funny. As one sportswriter wrote, it was "more fun losing with Stengel than winning with someone else." New York sportswriters enjoyed him, but he didn't seem serious enough to be the manager of the Yankees.

But Stengel was no dummy. He had been in baseball his entire life. He knew his players, and he knew how to win.

He proved it when the Yankees and the Red Sox resumed their rivalry in 1949. On paper, the Red Sox were the better team. The Yankees battled injuries all year long. DiMaggio, in particular, missed much of the year with a bone spur in his heel.

It didn't matter. Stengel always seemed to know whom to put in the lineup. The two teams were neck-and-neck for much of the season. Then, in September, Joe DiMaggio contracted pneumonia and was sidelined. The Red Sox pulled ahead by one.

Boston came into New York for the last two games of the season. To win the pennant, the Yankees needed to win both contests.

Joe DiMaggio was still weak from pneumonia, but he insisted on playing. The Sox led early on, 4–0, but the Yankees and DiMaggio didn't quit. In the fourth inning, the Yankee Clipper blasted a double that helped New York score twice. New York caught fire and stormed back to win, 5–4.

Now the two teams were tied for first place. The

final game of the regular season would decide the pennant.

This time the Yankees took a commanding 5–0 lead in the game, and the Red Sox staged a comeback that took them to within one. But in the end, they came up short; New York won, 5–4, and took the pennant.

They faced their crosstown rivals the Brooklyn Dodgers again in 1949. The Dodgers were determined to win this time, but the Yankees had all the momentum. New York rolled over Brooklyn in five games, and once again the Yankees were world champions.

On paper, the Yankees appeared unstoppable. Since 1921, they had been in 16 World Series and had won 12. Yet when the 1950 season got under way, all the experts picked the Red Sox to win the pennant. They pointed out that 36-year-old DiMaggio was slowing down and the Yankees didn't really have another big star.

That hardly mattered, however. The Yankee farm system was beginning to restock the club.

On opening day in Boston, the Red Sox jumped out to a 9–0 lead. Then the Yankees came pounding back to win the game, 15–10. That victory set the tone for the season.

That year saw the emergence of great new players. Catcher Yogi Berra, famous for his puzzling one-liners, emerged as a star; and shortstop Phil Rizzuto had the best season of his career, winning the American League's MVP award. Rookie pitcher Whitey Ford came up in midseason and went 9–1. With this talent, New York ended the season with a first-place record of 98 wins, 56 losses.

The Yankees faced the Philadelphia Phillies in the World Series. They won the first game by a single run.

Game two proved to the world that Joe DiMaggio still had plenty of "slug" left in him. The score had been tied 1–1 since the fifth inning. Then, at the top of the tenth, DiMaggio came to the plate — and walloped a pitch for a home run!

New York won that game, 2–1, and took the next two contests as well. The phrase "World Champion New York Yankees" was becoming commonplace.

The Yankees didn't mind. They liked the way that sounded, and wanted to hear it over and over again. But would they?

⋆ CHAPTER FIVE ⋆

1951–1964

End of an Era

As Joe DiMaggio began to slow down, Yankee fans anxiously began looking for the next Yankee legend. They didn't have very long to wait.

In 1949, Yankee scout Tom Greenwade had discovered a young prospect in rural Oklahoma. He later said that he felt like the Yankee scout who had first seen Lou Gehrig. The young man had as much raw talent as any prospect Greenwade had ever seen. As soon as he graduated from high school, the Yankees signed him.

His name was Mickey Mantle. A shortstop and switch-hitter, Mantle could hit with power and run like the wind. He had hit .383 in the minor leagues in 1950, but he had also made 55 errors.

Casey Stengel decided to test Mantle during spring training in 1951. He chose to take advantage of Mantle's speed and have him play outfield. Mantle hit nine home runs during spring training and made the team.

But after a quick start, the rookie slumped. Casey Stengel had no choice but to send him back to the minor leagues. Stengel still had faith in the 19-year-old, however. "He'll be back," he said, "and I'll bet you that when he does he won't go down anymore."

Yet Mantle's slump continued in the minor leagues. Then his father came for a visit. He told his son that if he didn't want to play, he should come home. Then he started packing Mickey's bag.

That woke up the younger Mantle fast! He stopped his father and soon started hitting. A few weeks later, Stengel called him back up to the majors; Mantle never looked back.

Mantle proved to be the spark the Yankees needed that season. They overtook Cleveland in the final weeks of the season and won the pennant yet again.

In 1951, their opponents in the World Series were the New York Giants. Like the Yankees, the Giants had a new outfielder who was loaded with talent. His name was Willie Mays; and like Mantle, he had given his team just the jolt they needed to win games.

The Giants also had plenty of momentum. They had won an amazing 37 of their final 44 games of the season and then beaten the Brooklyn Dodgers in a best-of-three series to win the pennant. They ran onto the field on October 4 determined to unseat the mighty Yankees.

It seemed their determination would pay off, too. They outhit the Yankees ten to seven to win the first game, 5–1.

But the next day, the Yankees batted in two early runs. By the top of the fifth inning, they looked unstoppable.

Willie Mays was up first that inning. He lofted a high fly ball toward right center field.

DiMaggio, playing center field, ran in to make the catch. So did Mickey Mantle. DiMaggio was in a better position, and normally Mantle wouldn't have chased down the ball. So why did he?

Some believe that Casey Stengel had been concerned that DiMaggio, once the best player on the field, was slowing down. He thought the center fielder might need some assistance, and so he told Mantle to "take everything he could." By going for the fly ball, Mantle was just following his manager's instructions.

Mantle realized that this time, however, DiMaggio didn't need any help. So he pulled up short. As he did, disaster struck. Mantle's right cleat stuck in an outfield drain cover, his knee wrenched horribly to one side, and he fell in a heap.

That was it for him that game, and for the remaining games of the World Series. Although he would eventually recover, the knee injury was the first of many that would dog Mantle throughout his career.

The Yankees managed to win game two without Mantle; and although they lost the next day, they went on to win three in a row to take their 14th World Series title.

A short time after the championship, Joe DiMaggio retired. In his 13 seasons in pinstripes, the Yankee Clipper's team had won ten pennants and nine World Series. They also won more than two-thirds of their games. Although many players had better personal statistics than DiMaggio, very few have helped their team win as much as he helped the Yankees.

But even without DiMaggio, the Yankees were almost unstoppable. They won pennants in six of the next seven seasons, missing out only in 1954 when they finished second to Cleveland. Mantle took over in center field for DiMaggio and immediately became the team's best and most popular player, cracking home runs and running the bases with abandon despite near-continuous pain in his legs.

Mantle had plenty of help, too. Whitey Ford emerged as one of the best pitchers in baseball. And behind home plate was the jug-eared, stocky catcher, Yogi Berra, whose talented play won him the American League's Most Valuable Player award in 1951, 1954, and 1955.

The Yankees weren't the only great New York team during the first half of the 1950s, however. Both the Giants and the Dodgers were also playing winning baseball. In fact, at least one New York team was in the World Series each year from 1950 to 1955. Not surprisingly, rivalry between the Giants, Dodgers, and Yankees was intense.

In 1955, the Yankees finally did something many thought was long overdue. Ever since Jackie Robinson had broken the color barrier in 1947, there had been calls for the Yankees to sign and play an African American player. Eight years later, the team decided Elston Howard was that player. He made the opening day roster and was a valuable player from the start, adding 81 hits, including ten home runs and seven triples in the 97 games he played that year.

The Yankees, too, got off to a good start. They put the Cleveland Indians, their primary rival that year, in their rearview mirror early on and then roared into the postseason with a record of 96 wins, 58 losses.

Meanwhile the Brooklyn Dodgers won the National League pennant with an even more impressive record of 98 wins, 55 losses — despite the fact that many of the Dodgers, such as Jackie Robinson, were approaching retirement. With the 1955 World Series shaping up to be the last chance for these players to finally beat the Yankees, the Dodgers came out swinging. They drove the Series to a three-to-three-game tie and then managed to eke out a two–nothing victory in the final game to wrest the championship from the rivals at last.

Then, unbelievably, both teams won the pennant again in 1956. New York baseball fans buzzed with excitement in the days before the World Series. Who, they asked, would win the rematch?

The Dodgers seemed to answer the question early on by winning both games. But the Yankees didn't quit. They won the next two games to tie the Series.

In game five, manager Casey Stengel decided to start pitcher Don Larsen. Only two years before, while playing for the Orioles, Larsen lost 21 games. After being traded to the Yankees, however, he'd pitched well. Late in the 1956 season he'd been New York's hottest pitcher, winning four straight games.

But the Dodgers' pitcher, Sal Maglie, was just as strong; and neither team got a hit in the first three innings. Then in the fourth inning, Maglie tried to sneak a fastball past Mickey Mantle. Mantle got a good look at the pitch and swung from his heels.

Crack!

The sound of bat hitting ball echoed through the park. The ball sailed over the right-field wall, and at last the Yankees were on the board. They scored again in the sixth, giving them the lead at 2–0.

Larsen, meanwhile, just kept pitching and getting batters out. Although he wasn't striking out many hitters, he was getting them to hit weak pop-ups and ground balls. By the bottom of the ninth inning, the scoreboard told an incredible story. Not a single Dodger hitter had reached first base. Don Larsen was pitching a perfect game.

No pitcher had ever thrown a no-hitter in the World Series, not to mention a perfect game. When he went to the mound in the ninth inning, the crowd was humming with anticipation. The hum grew to a roar when he retired the first two batters.

Then pinch hitter Dale Mitchell came to the plate. Larsen threw a ball, and then got two strikes on Mitchell. On the next pitch, Mitchell fouled.

Then, for the 97th time that day, Larsen peered in at Yogi Berra, took the sign, and threw. The pitch was above the waist and tailed away from Mitchell, who started to swing and then stopped.

Umpire Babe Pinelli didn't hesitate. His right hand shot into the air and he called out, "Strike three!"

Larsen had thrown the only perfect game in World Series history! Yogi Berra ran out to the mound and jumped into the grinning pitcher's arms. The rest of the Yankees followed close behind and mobbed their teammate.

That win spurred the Yankees on to victory twice more, giving them their 15th World Series championship. New York then won *another* pennant in 1957, but this time, they lost the Series to the Milwaukee Braves. In 1958 they beat the Braves in a rematch, but finished in third place in 1959 behind the first-place Chicago White Sox and second-place Cleveland Indians.

In the off-season, the Yankees acquired a promising player named Roger Maris. Maris had started off in the minor leagues six years earlier, and then played a year with the Cleveland Indians before being traded to the Kansas City Royals midseason his second year.

At the start of the 1960 season, he put on the Yankee pinstripes for the first time — and by the halfway point, he led the league in home runs with 27 and runs batted in with 69. He injured himself sliding into base and was sidelined for 17 games, yet still managed to make the All-Star team and to lead the league in RBIs.

Meanwhile, Mickey Mantle, Yogi Berra, Whitey Ford, and the rest of the Yankee lineup continued to deliver top-notch performances. To the surprise of no one, they ran away with the pennant six games ahead of the second-place Baltimore Orioles.

The Yankees played the Pittsburgh Pirates in the World Series. In games two, three, and six of the Series, they were devastating, crushing the Pirates, 16–3, 10–0, and 12–0.

The Pirates didn't roll over and play dead, however. They won games one, four, and five, forcing the Series into a seventh and final game.

It was a great game, as both teams traded the lead back and forth. In the bottom of the ninth, the game was tied, 9–9. Pittsburgh's first batter, Bill Mazeroski, came up to the plate. So far in the game, he had bunted a single, popped out to short, and grounded into a double play.

This time, he took his place in the history books, blasting the first-ever World Series walk-off home run. As the Pirates jumped and screamed with joy, the Yankees simply stood by, too shocked by the sudden turnaround to do anything more.

Despite the 1960 World Series upset, baseball watchers everywhere recognized that the Yankees were the dominant team in the sport, and had been for many years. They owed their success to great players, of course, but also to the leadership of Casey Stengel.

But Stengel was now 70 years old. Before the 1961 season, the Yankees' owners urged him to retire. Stengel wanted to continue managing; but finally, and with great reluctance, he agreed to step down. Ralph Houk, a former Yankee catcher, became the new manager.

The change in management became nothing more than a footnote in the Yankees' 1961 season, however. That year belonged to Roger Maris.

The previous season, Maris had taken a backseat to Mantle, in part because of his midseason injury and in part because Mantle was so clearly the favorite player on the team. Fans considered Maris a solid player but didn't expect him to break out of the field.

He seemed to live up to their expectations by getting off to a slow start in April. That month, he hit just a single home run.

In May, however, when he hit 11 homers, some baseball fans started to take notice. More turned their eyes to him in June, when he hit 15. And by the end of August, when his home-run mark stood at 50, anyone who followed baseball knew that Roger

Maris was on track to break Babe Ruth's single-season home-run record.

Mickey Mantle was also on pace to break Ruth's record. The two traded the home-run lead for much of the season. Then in September Mantle was sidelined with an illness. He finished with a remarkable 54 home runs.

Any other year, that number might have given him first place in the home-run standings. But not this year.

On September 26, 1961, Roger Maris tied Babe Ruth's record by hitting his 60th home run. He sat out the next game, but came to the plate again on the 29th. Unfortunately, that game he walked twice and popped out twice. The following day, he walked, grounded out twice, and hit a single.

The Yankees had one game left to play in the regular season. Maris had one last chance to beat Ruth's record.

Many people hoped Maris would fail. Even though Babe Ruth hadn't played for decades, he was still baseball's most beloved player. His 60-home-run record had stood since 1927; as far as fans were concerned, it deserved to stand for many years to come.

Babe Ruth, the most famous Yankee of all time, clouts one of the many home runs of his career.

July 4, 1939: An emotional Lou Gehrig delivers his farewell speech, his amazing career cut short by the ravages of ALS, otherwise known as Lou Gehrig's disease.

Slugger Joe DiMaggio blasts hit number 42 on his way to setting the 1941 record of 56 consecutive hits.

Switch-hitter Mickey Mantle belts a single during a game in 1956.

Catcher Yogi Berra leaps into the arms of pitcher Don Larsen after Larsen pitched a perfect game in the World Series, the first time any pitcher had accomplished this feat.

In the last game of the 1961 season, Roger Maris hits his 61st home run, breaking the record held by Babe Ruth since 1927.

Reggie Jackson watches his third consecutive World Series home run leave the park during Game 6 in 1977.

October 26, 2000: The New York Yankees celebrate their 26th World
Series victory!

Besides, a great number of people pointed out, even if Maris did hit another, it wasn't the same as what Ruth had done. Ruth had set his record in a 154-game season; Maris had the advantage of playing in a 162-game season.

Maris, meanwhile, was feeling so much pressure that his hair was falling out. He was so nervous that he barely slept.

On October 1, the Yankees faced the Red Sox in the final game of the regular season. The game was scoreless through three and a half innings. Then, in the bottom of the fourth, Maris came up to bat. There was one out, no one on base.

Boston pitcher Tracy Stallard took the signal and threw a fastball. The pitch was a little up, and a little in.

That's just right where Maris liked it.

He swung, using the same smooth stroke he had all year. He connected. The ball soared to right field in Yankee Stadium and then settled into a sea of hands six rows deep. Roger Maris had broken Babe Ruth's record!

That homer was the only run of the game. With the win, New York had its 109th victory of the season — and of course, the pennant.

With such a miracle season ender, the World Series was almost an afterthought. Despite the fact that Mantle was still hurt and barely played, the Yankees dispatched the Cincinnati Reds in five games. Maris hit a home run in game three, and the Yankees were world champs.

In 1962, Maris came back to earth, and ever so slowly, so did the rest of the Yankees. They would still enjoy several more relatively successful seasons, but in a sense this edition of the Yankees had peaked in 1961. The core of the team — Mantle, Maris, Ford, Howard, and Berra — would soon show signs of age.

Still, they won the Series yet again that year, but in 1963, it become clear that the Yankees were starting to slide. They stormed to another pennant all the same.

Their opponents in the World Series were the Los Angeles Dodgers (the Brooklyn team had been moved to California in 1958). That team was led by ace pitcher Sandy Koufax, whose record that year was 25 and 5. The Yankees entered the contest confident they could best Koufax but soon found that they were completely outmatched. As Yogi Berra said of Koufax afterward, "I see how he won 25 games. What I don't understand is how he lost five."

The Yankees' slow slide downhill continued in 1964. Ralph Houk was let go as manager and replaced by Yogi Berra. After a tough fight the team won another pennant but again lost the World Series, this time to the St. Louis Cardinals.

There was another development for the team that year, too. Near the end of the season the Yankees were purchased by the CBS television network. Many people thought the sale would start a new era in Yankee history.

It did, but in ways few people could ever have imagined.

★ CHAPTER SIX ★

1965–1974

Down and Out

The new Yankee owners were so impressed by the way the Cardinals played in the World Series that they fired Yogi Berra and hired the Cardinals' manager, Johnny Keene, to take over the Yankees. When the Yankees got off to a slow start in 1965, no one was worried. That had been their pattern for several seasons, but they had always gotten hot.

That never happened in 1965. Mantle, Maris, and Howard were all sidelined with injuries. The Yankees tried to make a few trades to acquire some replacements and bring up some younger players from the minor leagues, but the trades didn't work out and the rookies weren't ready. Over the years the Yankee minor-league system, which in the past had supplied great players year after year, had deteriorated. There were no great stars on the horizon.

For the first time in decades, the mighty Yankees lost more games than they won, finishing 77–85 to end up in sixth place. Yet instead of making any changes in 1966, the Yankees, as if not believing the standings, didn't do anything.

Incredibly, the Yankees were even worse in 1966. Keene was fired and Ralph Houk returned as manager in 1967, but he couldn't stop the Yankees' slide.

After years of success, Yankees fans had gotten spoiled. They were used to seeing All-Stars at almost every position. Now all they saw were a bunch of players who used to be good. Mickey Mantle was getting old and he limped around the outfield. Whitey Ford struggled to win. With no outstanding newcomers, Yankee games became depressing to watch.

By late September the Yankees were in last place. New York baseball fans turned their attention to the Mets. In one late-season game at Yankee Stadium, which could seat more than 70,000 people, only 413 fans showed up for the game. The Yankees ended the year with a record of 70–89, the worst team in the American League.

Over the next few seasons the Yankees scrambled

to return to their once unbeatable status. After Mantle and Ford retired in 1968, fans kept looking for the next Mantle or the next Ford to arrive.

But such players weren't easy to find. The Yankees weren't completely without talented players, as pitcher Mel Stottlemyre and outfielders Bobby Murcer and Roy White were stars, but they didn't have much help.

The Yankee owners themselves didn't help matters much. Since acquiring the team, CBS hadn't invested any money in the franchise. Other teams willing to spend were signing all the best young prospects. Yankee Stadium, once the greatest ballpark ever built, began to deteriorate, as did the area surrounding it. Many fans simply didn't feel safe going to Yankee Stadium. In the meantime, the New York Mets captured the attention of the whole city with a surprising pennant and world championship in 1969.

Then, just as the baseball world gave up on the Yankees, the team started to turn things around. Led by White and Murcer, the Yankees were surprisingly competitive in 1970 and won 93 games, finishing second. Over the next several seasons, although they failed to win 93 games again, they were at least respectable.

Still, Yankee fans simply weren't coming to Yankee Stadium. In fact, visitors were staying away from New York City completely. The city was in financial trouble, and the crime rate had skyrocketed while city services deteriorated.

Finally, in a move calculated to help the Yankees and New York City at the same time, the city agreed to buy Yankee Stadium and renovate it. The facelift would take two years and start in 1974. In the meantime, the Yankees would share Shea Stadium with the Mets.

After the deal was made, CBS decided to sell the Yankees. Unfortunately, there was very little interest in the team. Then a man no one had ever heard of stepped forward and put together a deal to buy the club.

His name was George Steinbrenner, a native of Cleveland who ran a Great Lakes shipping company. Steinbrenner had been trying to buy a baseball team for years. On January 4, 1973, he and a group of investors he'd put together finalized the deal. Steinbrenner indicated that he intended to stay behind the scenes, saying that he was far too busy running his businesses to take an active role in running the Yankees.

"I'd be silly trying to run the ball club, too," he said.

Over the next few decades sportswriters often reminded Steinbrenner of those words. Far from leaving the team for others to run, Steinbrenner became the most hands-on and influential owner in Yankee history.

Steinbrenner made an immediate impact on the team. First, he ordered all the Yankees with long hair to get haircuts and shave their beards. Then he helped make a few key trades, which not only added good players to the team but showed their willingness to spend money for talent.

In August, it appeared as if Steinbrenner's club would challenge for the division title. But the team faded over the final weeks. Meanwhile the Mets won another division title and world championship. Once again, the Yankees weren't even first in their own city.

More changes occurred after the 1973 season. Ralph Houk resigned, and the Yankees hired Bill

Virdon to be their new manager. Construction equipment moved into the Bronx to begin work on the stadium. The Yankees moved to Queens to share Shea Stadium with the Mets. Then Yankee general manager Gabe Paul began to rebuild the team. Almost every week or two he made another trade aimed at bolstering the lineup.

At first the changes seemed to throw the Yankees off balance. They fell into last place in July. But then, unbelievably, they roared back to life and took over first place in early September. They won 20 of their last 31 games, a performance that in most seasons would have resulted in a division title. But the Baltimore Orioles won 25 games during the same time period, including a three-game sweep of the Yankees. In the end, the Yankees finished second.

As soon as the 1974 season ended, Paul made another big trade. He sent longtime Yankee Bobby Murcer, a fan favorite, to the San Francisco Giants for Bobby Bonds. Bonds, the father of future slugger Barry Bonds, was a terrific player who not only hit for power but also stole bases and played a great center field.

Not long afterward, they made another addition

to the team. Star pitcher Catfish Hunter had played for the Oakland A's, but late in the 1975 season A's owner Charlie Finley missed a salary payment. That made Hunter a free agent, a player not under contract to any team. He was now free to join any team he wanted. He joined the Yankees.

A new era in Yankee history was about to start.

⋆ CHAPTER SEVEN ⋆

1975–1978

The Bronx Zoo

Despite the presence of Catfish Hunter, who would go on to win 23 games, not much went right for the Yankees in 1975. First, George Steinbrenner was convicted of making an illegal campaign contribution to a politician. Although he didn't have to go to jail, baseball suspended him for the season. Then several key players were hurt. In late July the Yankees fired manager Bill Virdon and hired a former Yankee infielder, fiery Billy Martin.

Martin loved to win, and he fought and scratched for every victory. He had a well-earned reputation as a manager that got the most out of his ball club. Even so, the many changes in 1975 had shaken the team. At season's end, they were only third in the standings.

Billy Martin didn't let up. The team moved back

into Yankee Stadium in 1976 and got off to a quick start — and didn't look back. Catfish Hunter won 25 games and for the first time since 1964, the Yankees won the division title. In the playoffs they played the scrappy Kansas City Royals. The two clubs split the first four games. The winner of game five would go on to the World Series.

In the ninth inning the score was tied, 6–6. Yankee first baseman Chris Chambliss stepped to the plate. Although Chambliss was hitting close to .300, he hadn't hit very many home runs. The crowd at Yankee Stadium was going crazy.

Kansas City pitcher Mark Littell wound up and threw. Chambliss swung.

Boom!

All of a sudden the ball was soaring through the air, one bright spot against the dark of night. Chambliss started running toward first; and when he saw the ball start to drop into the right-field stands, he started jumping as he ran. It was a home run! After years of dawdling in the cellar, the Yankees were returning to the World Series!

Hundreds of fans ran out on the field. By the time Chambliss rounded third base, he couldn't fight his way through the crowd to home plate. Fortunately, some New York City policemen helped him from the field; and later, after the field was cleared of fans, he was allowed to go back and touch home plate.

Unfortunately, the comeback story ended there. The Yankees played the Cincinnati Reds in the World Series. The Cincinnati team was nicknamed the Big Red Machine, and for good reason. With stars like Johnny Bench, Joe Morgan, and Pete Rose, the Reds had steamrolled over their competition on their way to the NL championship. In the World Series they just kept on motoring, dispatching the Yankees in a four-game sweep.

Yankee fans, players, and owners were disappointed not to have done better in their first Series in 12 years. But big changes were afoot to ensure they wouldn't be disappointed again.

In the off-season one of the greatest sluggers in the game, Reggie Jackson, became a free agent. Like Babe Ruth or Mickey Mantle, Jackson was a larger-than-life figure. When he stepped to the plate, everyone watched. He swung so hard that even when he missed it was exciting.

He also had a big ego. He was so cocky that some people thought he was obnoxious. One of his own teammates once said of him that "there's not enough mustard in the world to cover that hot dog."

Jackson knew that New York was the most exciting city in the major leagues. Several years before he had said, "If I played in New York, they'd name a candy bar after me."

George Steinbrenner decided to test that theory. He contacted the slugger and made him an offer. Even though the Montreal Expos offered him more money, Jackson signed with New York and donned Yankee pinstripes for the first time in 1977.

But not everyone welcomed Jackson. Manager Billy Martin resented him, and Jackson gave an interview in which he insulted Yankee captain Thurman Munson, saying, "I'm the straw that stirs the drink. . . . Munson can only stir it bad."

Clubhouse strife often leads to poor performance, and Jackson and the Yankees got off to a slow start. Then, in midseason, in a nationally televised game in Boston against the Red Sox, Jackson muffed a fly ball. Billy Martin replaced him in the middle of the game. He and Jackson argued in the dugout and nearly got into a fight. One of the Yankees termed the Yankee clubhouse the Bronx Zoo.

Incredibly, the Yankees were able to put the incident behind them and suddenly started playing better baseball. Jackson got hot; young pitcher Ron Guidry pitched great; and the Yankees raced to the division title. They defeated the Royals in the play-offs to make the Series for the second year in a row.

This time the Yankees faced the Dodgers in the World Series. Entering game six the Yankees led three games to two. One more victory would make them world champions.

Reggie Jackson had been playing well and had smacked two home runs, one in game four and another in his last at bat in game five. Still, no one was prepared for his performance in game six.

He walked his first at bat, but when he came to the plate the second time . . .

Smack!

. . . Jackson drove the ball into the right-field seats for a home run that put New York ahead 4–3. When Jackson got back in the dugout he looked at the camera and, in a gesture very much like Babe Ruth in the 1932 World Series, held up one finger.

"That's just one," the gesture seemed to say.

He came up to bat again an inning later. Once again he swung at the first pitch he saw and hit it square.

Boom!

The ball rocketed into the right-field stands for his second home run. This time when he got to the dugout he held up two fingers. Those two, plus the homer he'd hit his last at bat in game three, had Jackson hitting three home runs in three swings!

When Reggie came to bat again in the eighth inning, Yankee fans were on their feet, chanting "Reggie! Reggie! Reggie!" Everyone was wondering if he could hit another home run.

This time he faced veteran knuckleball pitcher Charlie Hough. Knuckleballs are thrown slowly and dance through the air. They are very difficult to hit cleanly.

Hough's first pitch floated over the plate. Jackson swung from his heels. For the third time that day, the sound of his bat meeting the ball echoed through the ballpark.

The ball took off toward center field. Jackson stood at the plate for a moment watching. And then he slowly started jogging to first.

Fans saw the ball go up and up, and then start to drop down. It finally clattered to earth far beyond the center-field fence for one of the longest home runs in the history of Yankee Stadium. Jackson had hit four home runs on four swings in the World Series, three in one game!

As smooth as ever, Jackson held up three fingers when he got to the dugout.

Even the Dodgers were impressed. First baseman Steve Garvey later admitted that after Jackson's third home run, he had clapped for the Yankee. New York won the game, and the World Series, and Jackson earned a new nickname. The press started calling him Mr. October.

In the off-season, Reggie's prediction of long ago came true. A candy company began manufacturing a candy bar called "Reggie!" Thousands were given away on opening day at Yankee Stadium in 1978. Unfortunately, thousands were thrown back onto the field.

It was a bad omen.

Early in the season nothing went right. The Yankees weren't hitting, and every pitcher except Ron Guidry had a sore arm.

Almost by himself, Guidry kept the Yankees above .500. Although Guidry wasn't very big, he threw hard and his slider was almost unhittable. On June 17 he set a club record with 18 strikeouts in one game.

But he couldn't pitch every game. The Yankees were losing, and everyone was on edge. Martin and Jackson clashed again when Reggie tried to bunt after Martin ordered him to swing away. Jackson was fined and left the team. When George Steinbrenner appeared to back Jackson, Martin said that Jackson and the owner "deserve each other. One's a born liar, the other's convicted." Steinbrenner was sensitive about his criminal record and he fired Martin, replacing him with Bob Lemon, who was as calm and relaxed as Martin was intense and emotional.

Once again, clubhouse infighting seemed about to destroy the Yankees' chances that season. In fact, at one time the Red Sox led the Yankees by 14 games in the race for the division title. No one thought the Yankees had a chance.

But all of a sudden the Yankee players stopped grumbling and started playing. Injured pitchers got healthy, and for the rest of 1978 the Yankees were almost unstoppable. The Red Sox, meanwhile, went into a tailspin. In early September the Yankees swept the Red Sox in a four-game series to pull to within a game of first place, outscoring them, 42–9, in what sportswriters called the Boston Massacre.

The two teams finished the season tied for first place. To decide the divisional title they met in a one-game playoff at Fenway Park. Ron Guidry started the game for the Yankees while Mike Torrez, a one-time Yankee, pitched for the Red Sox.

Entering the seventh inning, the Yankees trailed. The first two batters singled. Then, after a fly out, New York shortstop Bucky Dent stepped to the plate.

Dent was in a terrible slump. For his last 20 games his batting average was only .140. Now he fell behind in the count, and then fouled a ball off his foot.

The game was delayed while the Yankees' trainer attended to him. Dent couldn't leave the game — the Yankees had no one else to play shortstop.

During the delay, another Yankee noticed that Dent's bat was chipped and gave him another. Then Dent stepped back into the batter's box.

Mike Torrez hadn't thrown a pitch the whole time he was waiting. Now he threw one to Dent.

The shortstop chopped at the ball, and it flew to left field. Fenway Park's left-field fence — also known as the Green Monster — isn't very far from home plate. But it is 37 feet high. Red Sox left fielder Carl Yastrzemski started drifting back toward the wall. He thought Dent's hit was a routine fly ball.

It wasn't. Yastrzemski stopped moving and looked up as Dent's little fly ball ducked over the wall into the net that kept home runs from falling into the street.

Home run? *Home run!* The Yankees couldn't believe it. The three-run homer put them ahead. Two innings later, Yankee reliever Goose Gossage struck out Yastrzemski for the final out of the game. The Yankees won, 5–4, to take the division.

For the third year in a row, they beat the Kansas City Royals in the playoffs. They then faced the Dodgers in the World Series for the second time in as many years.

After dropping the first two games, it appeared as if the Yankees would lose this time around. But these Yankees had been coming back all year long. They hadn't quit when they had trailed the Red Sox by 14 games, and they weren't going to quit now.

In game three third baseman Graig Nettles made one spectacular stop after another, saving at least five runs to help the Yankees win, 5–1. Then in game four, with the Yankees trailing 3–1 in the sixth inning, Reggie Jackson was hit by a throw while running the bases. Another Yankee came around and scored to pull to within one run. They later won the game to tie the Series.

Now the momentum was on New York's side. In games five and six backup infielder Brian Doyle, playing in place of injured second baseman Willie Randolph, and the rejuvenated Bucky Dent each hammered Dodger pitching. The Yankees swept to victory. After the series, Doyle said, "I feel like Cinderella."

So did the Yankees' fans. Unfortunately, the clock was about to strike midnight.

☀ CHAPTER EIGHT ☀

1979–1995

Rebuilding

Although people criticized the Yankees for being the "best team money could buy," it was hard to argue with the results. After winning two consecutive world championships, the Yankees seemed poised to win more.

But the Yankees failed to realize that their recent success had as much to do with playing together as a team as it did about money. Over the next few years the team that seemed ready to become a dynasty would, instead, become a disappointment.

Steinbrenner had previously announced that Billy Martin would return as manager in 1980. But when the Yankees got off to a slow start under Bob Lemon in 1979, Lemon was fired and Martin was hired back a year early. Then tragedy struck.

Yankee captain and catcher Thurman Munson had recently acquired his pilot's license so he could spend more time with his family. On August 2, he was practicing takeoffs and landings in his new plane. But during one landing the plane lost power, skidded off the end of the runway, and burst into flames. Munson was killed.

The Yankees never got over the loss. They finished the 1980 season in fourth place.

In the off-season, Billy Martin let his fiery temper get away with him and got in a fight with a marshmallow salesman. Steinbrenner fired him again, replacing him with coach Dick Howser. At the same time, the Yankees made a slew of trades and free-agent signings. By spring training, they were an entirely different team.

Fortunately, Howser was a calming influence and got the team to play together. Reggie Jackson had his best year ever, hitting .300 and cracking 41 home runs. The Yankees won the division with 103 victories and prepared to face the Royals in the playoffs for the fourth time.

For Kansas City, four was their magic number.

Fourth playoff meeting. Four games. Four wins. The Yankees were out before they had a chance to get started.

George Steinbrenner was angry. He believed that unless the Yankees won the World Series, the season was a waste. He wanted Howser to fire some of his coaches. When the manager refused, Steinbrenner fired him. General manager Gene Michael became the manager.

Steinbrenner also decided that the Yankees needed to groom a new star to take over for the aging Reggie Jackson. San Diego outfielder Dave Winfield was a free agent. An incredible athlete, Winfield went from college straight to the major leagues without playing a minute in the minor leagues. He had also been drafted by the NBA and the NFL. Steinbrenner outbid several teams, and Winfield became a Yankee in 1981.

That season was marred by a player strike that started on June 12 and lasted until July 31. Hundreds of games were canceled, millions of dollars were lost, and countless fans felt betrayed.

Major-league owners then made an unusual decision to split the season into two halves. The number-one teams in each division prestrike would then play the number-one teams poststrike to determine the division champs.

The Yankees were the top-ranked team of the American League East for the first half; the Milwaukee Brewers took that spot for the second half. When the two met for the playoff, the Brewers' record was three wins better than the Yankees'. But that didn't matter. The Yankees beat them three games to two to advance to the AL Championship Series. In that contest, they swept the Oakland A's in three straight games. Once again, the Yankees were going to the World Series. But after winning the first two games, the Yankees lost the next four. Dave Winfield had a terrible Series, getting only one hit, and Steinbrenner himself embarrassed the Yankees by getting into a fight with a fan.

The Yankees were changing. In the off-season Reggie Jackson left as a free agent and Steinbrenner kept changing managers, finally settling on an old favorite, Billy Martin.

The Yankee players couldn't keep up with the ever-changing managers. While some players such as Dave Winfield, Rob Guidry, and youthful pitcher

Dave Righetti had promising seasons, the team finished in fifth place in 1982 and in third place in 1983. Steinbrenner fired Martin once again and in 1984 named Yogi Berra the Yankees' manager.

That year also saw the rise of another young Yankee. Nearly 500 players had been drafted ahead of Don Mattingly in 1979 before the Yankees picked him. They never expected him to be great, but he proved them wrong. At each stop in his minor-league career, he hit the ball consistently while impressing the organization with his heads-up play.

In 1984 he played his way into the Yankee lineup. Unlike Reggie Jackson or other Yankees stars who sported big egos, Mattingly cared only about baseball. Kirby Puckett of the Minnesota Twins captured Mattingly perfectly when he called him Donnie Baseball. Over the next five seasons Mattingly hit for a .325 batting average and averaged 27 home runs, 42 doubles, and 114 RBIs each season. In 1984 he won the batting titles and in 1985 was named American League MVP.

Yet despite Dave Winfield and Don Mattingly, the Yankees just couldn't win. They scored plenty of runs but never had enough pitching to finish in first place.

There were constant shake-ups to the club, too, for almost every year the Yankees seemed to bring in a whole new group of players and a new manager. The best free agents began to avoid the Yankees.

As a result, the Yankees kept coming close but just missing the playoffs. From 1984 through 1988 they won at least 85 games each season, but never finished in first place or made the postseason. Once beloved in their hometown, the Yankees were losing fans to the New York Mets, who won the World Series in 1986 over the Boston Red Sox.

The downslide continued in 1989 with the Yankees finishing below .500. Then, in 1990, George Steinbrenner was once again suspended from baseball. He was embroiled in a contract dispute with Dave Winfield and made the bad choice to have someone investigate the player. Yankee fans, tired of Steinbrenner's antics and of supporting a losing club, cheered when his suspension was announced at Yankee Stadium.

The ball club completely collapsed that year. They finished with a record of 67–95, their worst record since 1913. Even Don Mattingly played poorly. He hurt his back and was never the same player.

In the long run, however, the loss of Steinbrenner worked out for the best. One reason the Yankees hadn't won in recent years was because they usually traded their best prospects for veterans. But during his suspension, Steinbrenner wasn't allowed to have anything to do with the Yankees. The team decided to build for the future, and by 1992, their efforts started to pay off.

That year, new manager Buck Showalter was at the helm. Showalter had managed in the Yankees' minor-league system. He had faith in the team's younger players, like outfielder Bernie Williams and pitcher Andy Pettitte. These youngsters were supplemented by veterans like outfielder Paul O'Neill, pitcher Jimmy Key, and third baseman Wade Boggs. When George Steinbrenner's suspension ended in 1993, the Yankees were on their way to being respectable again and, by 1994, seemed a shoo-in for the playoffs.

Then season disaster struck in the form of a labor dispute between the players and the owners. While the two sides battled, baseball ground to a halt. Eventually, the remaining games of season and then the World Series were canceled.

In 1995 the baseball strike ended and baseball changed the rules. Instead of two divisions in each league, each league now had three divisions. Each division champion would make the playoffs as well as the team in each league with the next best record, a "wild-card" team.

For the first half of the 1995 season the Yankees struggled. Then in midseason pitcher David Cone became available. The Yankees made a trade for him and also added former Mets slugger Darryl Strawberry. Although Strawberry had battled alcohol and drug problems, when he was healthy he was still a terrific hitter.

Cone and Strawberry made a big difference. In the last six weeks of the season the Yankees put on a charge. They didn't win the division, but they did earn a playoff spot as the wild-card team.

No one was happier than Don Mattingly. He was thinking about retiring due to his bad back, but he'd never had a chance to play in the postseason. Now he was getting his chance.

The Yankees faced the Seattle Mariners, the champions of the American League's western division. With ace fastball pitcher Randy Johnson and outfielder Ken Griffey Junior, the Mariners were a terrific team.

The first two games were played at Yankee Stadium. In the first game the Yankees pounded Seattle, 9–6. The second game lasted an exhausting fifteen innings before Jim Leyritz of the Yankees hit a dramatic home run for the win.

Unfortunately, now the Yankees had to travel to Seattle. In their hometown the Mariners played much tougher, winning the next two games to set up a game-five showdown.

David Cone gave it everything he had, but in the eighth inning, after throwing almost 150 pitches, he ran out of steam. Seattle hit him hard enough to tie the game and send it into extra innings.

Because of the fifteen-inning game, both teams were just about out of pitchers. The Mariners were using starting pitcher Randy Johnson in relief while the Yankees were doing the same with starter Jack McDowell. New York went ahead in the top of the eleventh inning, but in the bottom of the inning Joey Cora and Ken Griffey singled. Then Edgar Martinez ripped a double.

Griffey outran the throw to the plate, sliding

across home with the winning run. The Yankees lost, and Don Mattingly's career was over. He had finished with a flourish, however, hitting .417 in the series with ten hits and six RBIs, even smacking four doubles and a home run.

After a long dry spell, the Yankees were finally back where they belonged, in the postseason. Over the next few years, they would make that an annual occurrence.

⋆ CHAPTER NINE ⋆

1996–2000

Return of the Dynasty

Even though the Yankees had made it back to the playoffs, in the off-season Steinbrenner demanded that manager Buck Showalter change his coaching staff. Showalter refused and instead resigned. Now the Yankees needed a new manager.

Many people were surprised when Joe Torre was introduced as the new Yankee skipper. As a catcher and third baseman, Torre had been a star with the Braves, the Cardinals, and the Mets. As a manager, however, he hadn't done very well. During five years with the Mets, he'd never had a winning record. As manager of the Braves he had won a divisional title in his first season, but it had gone downhill after that. His last managerial assignment with St. Louis had also been a disappointment. When he was hired, one New York newspaper ran a headline that called him Clueless Joe.

The other big change took place at shortstop. Ever since Bucky Dent had retired, the Yankees had never found an adequate shortstop. Dozens of players had played the position for the Yankees, but none had succeeded.

In 1991, however, the Yankees drafted a young shortstop named Derek Jeter. Jeter's grandmother was a big Yankee fan, and he had grown up one as well. Ever since he was a little boy, whenever anyone asked him what he wanted to be, he answered, "Shortstop for the New York Yankees."

He'd done well in three minor-league seasons, but in 1995 no one thought he was ready for the big leagues yet. However, Joe Torre liked what he saw of Jeter during spring training. When veteran shortstop Tony Fernandez broke his wrist, Jeter got his dream job.

From the very first game, he played as if he had an appointment with the Hall of Fame. On opening day the Yankees played the Cleveland Indians, and in the second inning Jeter made a magnificent over-the-shoulder catch of a pop-up. Later in the game he added a home run to help the Yankees cruise to a 7–1 win. The Yankees and Derek Jeter were on their way — and they never looked back.

New York outlasted Baltimore to win the division title and then beat the Texas Rangers in the divisional series to reach the AL championships. Meanwhile, the wild-card Baltimore beat Cleveland in the first round to win the right to play the Yankees.

In game one the Orioles seemed to be in command. With a 4–2 lead, they turned the game over to their ace closer, Armando Benitez.

Derek Jeter came to the plate. There was one out. Jeter took Benitez's pitch and lofted a fly ball to right field.

Outfielder Tony Tarasco drifted back up against the wall and prepared to make the catch. But as he reached for the ball, another hand reached out above the wall and swiped at it! The ball bounced into the stands.

A home run for Derek Jeter!

Tarasco pointed to the stands, claiming that a fan had interfered with the play. Tarasco was right, but the umpires disagreed. A 12-year-old boy, Jeffrey

Maier, had reached out over the fence to try to catch Jeter's hit and had accidentally knocked the ball into the stands.

The home run tied the game and sent it into extra innings. Bernie Williams finally ended the game with a home run to give the Yankees the win. New York then went on to win the pennant and reach the World Series for the first time since 1981.

Their opponents were the powerful Atlanta Braves, who won the first two games easily.

Joe Torre didn't panic, however. "We'll take three games in Atlanta and then come back and win it here," he said before the Yankees left New York.

Amazingly enough, that's just what happened. The Yankees stormed back to win three straight games in Atlanta, returning the Series to New York.

Now there was no stopping them. In the third inning they exploded for three runs and then turned the game over to their bull pen in the sixth inning. Four pitchers combined to shut the Braves down. When the Braves' Mark Lemke lifted a pop fly that settled in the glove of Yankee third baseman Charlie Hayes with two outs in the ninth inning, the Yankees were the champions of the world for the first time since 1978. As the players ran out onto the field and formed a big knot in the center of the diamond, a capacity crowd at Yankee stadium stood and cheered.

The Yankees set their sights on repeating as champions but found that difficult. Nothing went right in 1997, as several players were dogged by injuries. When the season ended, the Yankees held the wild card. Unfortunately, they fell in the playoffs to Cleveland.

In 1998 the Yankees and Steinbrenner were determined to make a comeback. Several trades and free-agent signings dramatically changed the lineup.

Still, the Yankees started slowly, winning only one of their first five games. Some sportswriters thought George Steinbrenner was going to fire Joe Torre.

After the Yankees' fourth loss, however, Torre held a meeting and chewed out the team but good. He knew they were a much better ball club than they had been showing, and he wanted them to improve.

They did. The next day they won, 13–8. Then they won the next day. And the next day. On April 21, the Yankees moved into first place and didn't look back.

One reason was the pitching staff. Andy Pettitte, David Cone, and David Wells were all terrific, and closer Mariano Rivera was the best in the game. Then in midseason, the Yankees signed Orlando Hernandez, a fantastic Cuban pitcher who had recently come to the United States. He made the Yankees even better. By July their record was 56–20, ten games ahead of second-place Boston.

The Yankees just kept winning and winning. No one could stop them. At the end of the season their record was an incredible 114–48, the most wins by any major-league team since 1906.

The Yankees were a machine in the postseason as well. In the playoffs they beat the Rangers in three straight games and then dumped Cleveland in six games to reach the World Series. Against such momentum, the San Diego Padres didn't have a chance. The Yankees swept that team as they had so many others that season. Once again, they were world champs — and had the best record in major-league history to boot.

"I don't know how you can't say we're the greatest team ever," said Jeter. "We won 125 games." Few people argued with him.

In 1999 the Yankees tried to get even better by trading David Wells for Roger Clemens, one of the greatest pitchers in baseball. Some people thought they'd win 130 games or more.

That didn't happen, but the Yankees were still pretty good. It took them a while to get going, however, because at the beginning of the season Joe Torre was sidelined with prostate cancer and Clemens struggled. Nevertheless the Yankees won another division championship and pennant, beating Texas and Boston in the playoffs.

They then took on the Atlanta Braves in the World Series. Anyone expecting a close match was disappointed, for the Yankees swept the Braves in four straight games to win their second consecutive world championship. They were the first team since the 1938–39 Yankees to sweep the World Series in back-to-back seasons.

By now, people were beginning to wonder if any team could beat the Yankees. For an answer, they had to look no farther than the Yankees' own backyard.

After several losing seasons the New York Mets were rapidly improving. In 1999 they had made the playoffs but lost to Atlanta. In 2000 they were determined to make it to the World Series. New York baseball fans dreamed of a so-called Subway Series between the Mets and the Yankees.

They got their wish as each club won the pennant. New York City hadn't been so excited by a World Series in decades. Not since 1956 had two New York teams met in the World Series.

In game one the Mets appeared to have the win in hand. With runner Timo Perez on first base, third baseman Todd Zeile hit a ball deep to left field.

Perez thought the ball was going to be a home run and started jogging. But it hit the top of the wall and fell back into play. Yankee outfielder David Justice gunned the ball back to the infield as Perez, seeing the ball in play, began running hard. It looked as if he would still score easily.

No one told Derek Jeter that, however. Justice's throw was off-line; but Jeter raced after it, caught the ball, and then leapt and threw home in one motion. The ball beat Perez to the plate, and Jorge Posada tagged him out.

That spectacular play changed the momentum of the game. The contest went into extra innings and in the twelfth, the Yankees stole the win, 4–3.

Roger Clemens started game two for the Yankees.

97

Earlier in the season, when the two teams met in interleague play, Clemens had hit Mets catcher Mike Piazza in the head with a pitch. Piazza thought it was on purpose and was determined to get revenge.

In the first inning, Piazza came to bat and swung at a pitch from Clemens. Then Piazza's bat broke in two. One part bounded toward Clemens. Clemens fielded it as if it were the ball — and then threw it away as if he had just realized what it really was. The thrown portion almost hit Piazza.

The two players started yelling at each other, and for a moment it looked as if they might fight. Fortunately, they didn't, but the incident seemed to take all the wind out of the Mets' sails. The Yankees won the Subway Series in five games.

With four World Championships in five seasons, there was no question that these New York Yankees were one of the best teams in baseball history. The only question that remained was how much longer they could keep it up.

✶ CHAPTER TEN ✶

2001–2006

Pinstripe Pride

At first, the 2001 season unfolded similarly to the 2000 season. The Yankees struggled early and then started playing better in midseason. In the beginning of September, they swept Boston in three games to secure the division title. By then, everyone figured the World Series would take place in the Bronx again.

Then everything — not just in baseball, but the world itself — changed. On September 11, terrorists flew two airplanes into the Twin Towers of the World Trade Center. The buildings soon collapsed and over 3,000 people were killed.

New York came to a standstill. All of a sudden baseball didn't seem very important.

The attacks, which also included a third plane that hit the Pentagon and a fourth that crashed in Pennsylvania, had a terrible impact on the inhabitants of the United States. In a world gone insane, they craved a return to normalcy. On September 17, Major League Baseball took a first step in that direction, with the resumption of the baseball season.

The Yankees won their first postattack home game on September 25. With that victory, they clinched the division title — and gave their fans something to smile about again.

In the first round of the playoffs the Yankees faced the Oakland A's. Despite New York's strong showing in recent years, few people gave the Yankees a chance. The A's had won 102 games while the Yankees were still distracted by the events of 9/11 and the fact that several players were injured. When the A's won the first two games, the Yankees looked as though they were finished.

But in game three Derek Jeter gave fans a reason to believe in their team.

It was the seventh inning. The Yankees were leading 1–0 with two outs when the A's Jeremy Giambi singled. Then Terrence Long hit a double into the right-field corner.

Yankee outfielder Shane Spencer fielded the ball and threw toward home. But the ball went over the heads of both cutoff men, Yankee second baseman Alfonso Soriano and first baseman Tino Martinez. Giambi raced toward home with the tying run.

All of a sudden Derek Jeter came from nowhere, streaking across the field. He grabbed the errant throw on the fly and shoveled the ball toward home plate. Jorge Posada made the catch and tagged a startled Giambi, who didn't slide.

"Out!" the umpire yelled.

Yankee Stadium exploded. No one had ever seen such a play before. As Yankee third baseman Scott Brosius said, "You don't practice the 'run toward the dugout and make a backhanded flip to the catcher' play."

The Yankees held on to win the game and then blasted the A's in the final two of the series. The victory gave them momentum entering the ALCS, where they faced the Seattle Mariners. Only three seasons after the Yankees had won 114 regular season games, the Mariners won 116.

That didn't matter to the Yankees. New York beat the Mariners in five games to reach the World Series again.

Yankee fans were ecstatic. Despite the sadness

that still enveloped the city as thousands of people worked 24 hours a day to recover victims at Ground Zero, every evening the Yankees were providing a little bit of relief.

Meanwhile, the Arizona Diamondbacks had won the National League pennant. They were a terrific team, paced by pitchers Randy Johnson and Curt Schilling. The Series opened in Arizona and the Diamondbacks, behind Schilling and Johnson, won the first two games.

Back in New York for game three, however, it was a different story. For three nights in a row the Yankees gave New York fans some unforgettable memories. For a few hours, it was almost possible to forget what had happened on September 11.

In the third meeting, the Yankees won a tight ball game, 2–1, with third baseman Scott Brosius knocking the winning hit in the seventh inning. Then, in game four, Arizona led 3–1 entering the ninth inning. With one out, Yankee outfielder Paul O'Neill, who had announced that he was retiring after the Series, punched a single into left field.

That brought up Tino Martinez. Relief pitcher Byung-Hyun Kim threw one pitch. Martinez swung.

All of a sudden the ball was soaring through the air to deep right field. Every fan in the stadium stood and cheered. The stands rocked and shook like never before as Martinez's drive flew over the fence for a home run. The game was tied, 3–3.

For the next three innings both teams threatened, but neither could score. It was after midnight when Derek Jeter came to the plate in the twelfth inning. He worked the count to 3–2 and then swung.

Boom! Jeter's hit soared over the right-field fence for a home run to give the Yankees a 4–3 win. Jeter raised his fist in triumph as he ran around the bases. The Series was tied.

Incredibly, game five was just as exciting. Once again, Arizona led by two runs entering the ninth inning, and once again their closer, Kim, was on the mound. With Jorge Posada on second base, Scott Brosius came to bat.

Yankee fans crossed their fingers and wished that Brosius would do what Jeter had done the night before. Their wish came true. Brosius cracked a home run to tie the game. Then once again, in the twelfth inning, the Yankees scored another run to tie the game, this time on a hit by Alfonso Soriano. Over three incredible nights of baseball, the Yankees had given New York fans something to believe in.

Unfortunately, when the Series returned to Arizona, the magic that marked the games in New York disappeared. The Diamondbacks blasted the Yankees, 15–2, in game six, and then, in game seven, the Yankees lost in the final inning as Mariano Rivera made a rare error that led to the winning run. Yet even though the Diamondbacks won the series, the Yankees had given their fans an unforgettable experience.

By now, the baseball world recognized that the Yankees were one of the best teams in the league. Each season, they expected great things from the team.

Over the next few years, the Yankees made a habit of coming close but falling short. In 2002 they won the division title, but fell to the Anaheim Angels in the playoffs. In 2003 they outlasted the Boston Red Sox in the regular season to win another division title. They then beat the Minnesota Twins in the first round of the playoffs. Now they would face the wild-card Red Sox in the ALCS.

Rivalry between the two clubs had always been fierce, and this year was no exception. Throughout the season the two teams had played each other hard, and that same style of play unfolded in the playoffs.

After six hard-fought games the series was tied. Then, in game seven, the Red Sox led, 5–2, with only two innings remaining.

But the Yankees refused to quit. First Jeter doubled off of ace pitcher Pedro Martinez. Then Bernie Williams singled. Up came Hideki Matsui, a recent acquisition from Japan. Matsui doubled to drive in Jeter. Now the Yankees were within a run. And they weren't through. Jorge Posada singled to center field, and the Yankees tied the game.

The score was still tied three innings later when Yankee third baseman Aaron Boone stepped to the plate. Since coming to the Yankees in midseason, Boone had struggled, barely hitting .200. But on the first pitch of the eleventh inning, Red Sox pitcher Tim Wakefield threw a knuckleball that didn't knuckle.

Boone swung from his heels and hit the ball square. It sailed up and out into the stands and sent the Yankees back to the World Series.

The Yankees were a big favorite to beat the Florida Marlins. But many of the players were spent after the emotional series with the Sox. The Marlins won in six games.

As usual, the Yankees tried hard to improve in the off-season. First off, they needed to find a new third baseman to replace Boone, who had broken his leg. Texas shortstop Alex Rodriguez became available in trade — but New York already had a star shortstop with Derek Jeter. Fortunately, they were able to convince "A-Rod" to move to third base. Many expected Rodriguez, arguably the best player in baseball, to lead the Yankees to the World Series.

But the 2004 season belonged to the Red Sox. For years, Boston had been a "close but no cigar" team, often losing out to the Yankees. Now, die-hard fans finally got some revenge on New York.

It didn't seem as if they would at first, however. The Yankees once again won the division titles, and they again met the Red Sox in the ALCS. New York swept the first three games, winning 10–7, 3–1, and then blasting the Red Sox 19–8 to take a commanding 3–0 lead in the playoffs.

Since no team in baseball history had ever lost a World Series after leading three games to none, many Yankee fans were already celebrating their team's victory. They soon learned that there is a first time for everything.

Unbelievably, Boston stormed back to win the next four games and the pennant. As the stunned Yankees headed home to lick their wounds, the Red Sox continued on to the World Series, which they won for the first time in 86 years.

In 2005 the Yankees regrouped and won the division title for the eighth straight season. Unfortunately they again bowed out in the playoffs, losing to the Los Angeles Angels in five games. The following season found them in the top once more, at least at the end of the regular season. But in the postseason, they fell short, losing to the Detroit Tigers three games to one.

Yankee players and fans alike were disappointed that the team didn't do better. But on October 11, 2006, their disappointment turned to horror when word got out that a small plane had crashed into a building in New York City. Fears that terrorists were again attacking the city were quickly laid to rest — but then the real story emerged.

The plane had been carrying two people. One was a 26-year-old flight instructor named Tyler Stanger. The other was Yankee pitcher Cory Lidle. Both had been killed immediately in the crash.

The news of Lidle's death saddened the baseball world tremendously. Although he had worn pinstripes for only a few months, he had played in the major leagues since 1997 and was well liked and respected as a player and a person.

Yankee first baseman Jason Giambi had been Lidle's friend for many years. "Right now," he said after hearing the news, "I am really in a state of shock, as I am sure the entire MLB family is. . . . I have known Cory and his wife, Melanie, for over 18 years and watched his son grow up. We played high school ball together and have remained close throughout our careers. We were excited to be reunited in New York this year and I am just devastated."

Sadly, tragedy such as Lidle's death is only too familiar to the Yankees and their fans. But if they have learned anything about their team, it is that the Yankees never quit.

Each season they try to win the World Series, and each season, they try to get better. Year after year they have treated their fans to spectacular memories and produced some of the greatest players in baseball history. Babe Ruth, Lou Gehrig, Joe DiMaggio, Mickey Mantle, and Derek Jeter have worn the Yankee pinstripes with pride.

Just who will be the next star Yankee is unknown, but one thing is for sure: The greatest team in baseball history is determined to remain the greatest.

New York Yankees Regular Season Results

Year	W	L	Pct	GB
2006	97	65	.599	—
2005	95	67	.586	—
2004	101	61	.623	—
2003	101	61	.623	—
2002	103	58	.640	—
2001	95	65	.594	—
2000	87	74	.540	—
1999	98	64	.605	—
1998	114	48	.704	—
1997	96	66	.593	2.0
1996	92	70	.568	—
1995	79	65	.549	7.0
1994	70	43	.619	—
1993	88	74	.543	7.0
1992	76	86	.469	20.0
1991	71	91	.438	20.0
1990	67	95	.414	21.0
1989	74	87	.460	14.5
1988	85	76	.528	3.5
1987	89	73	.549	9.0
1986	90	72	.556	5.5
1985	97	64	.602	2.0
1984	87	75	.537	17.0
1983	91	71	.562	7.0
1982	79	83	.488	16.0

Year	W	L	Pct	GB
1981	59	48	.551	2.0
1980	103	59	.636	—
1979	89	71	.556	13.5
1978	100	63	.613	—
1977	100	62	.617	—
1976	97	62	.610	—
1975	83	77	.519	12.0
1974	89	73	.549	2.0
1973	80	82	.494	17.0
1972	79	76	.510	6.5
1971	82	80	.506	21.0
1970	93	69	.574	15.0
1969	80	81	.497	28.5
1968	83	79	.512	20.0
1967	72	90	.444	20.0
1966	70	89	.440	26.5
1965	77	85	.475	25.0
1964	99	63	.611	—
1963	104	57	.646	—
1962	96	66	.593	—
1961	109	53	.673	—
1960	97	57	.630	—
1959	79	75	.513	15.0
1958	92	62	.597	—
1957	98	56	.636	—
1956	97	57	.630	—
1955	96	58	.623	—

Year	W	L	Pct	GB
1954	103	51	.669	8.0
1953	99	52	.656	—
1952	95	59	.617	—
1951	98	56	.636	—
1950	98	56	.636	—
1949	97	57	.630	—
1948	94	60	.610	2.5
1947	97	57	.630	—
1946	87	67	.565	17.0
1945	81	71	.533	6.5
1944	83	71	.539	6.0
1943	98	56	.636	—
1942	103	51	.669	—
1941	101	53	.656	—
1940	88	66	.571	2.0
1939	106	45	.702	—
1938	99	53	.651	—
1937	102	52	.662	—
1936	102	51	.667	—
1935	89	60	.597	3.0
1934	94	60	.610	7.0
1933	91	59	.607	7.0
1932	107	47	.695	—
1931	94	59	.614	13.5
1930	86	68	.558	16.0
1929	88	66	.571	18.0
1928	101	53	.656	—

Year	W	L	Pct	GB
1927	110	44	.714	—
1926	91	63	.591	—
1925	69	85	.448	28.5
1924	89	63	.586	2.0
1923	98	54	.645	—
1922	94	60	.610	—
1921	98	55	.641	—
1920	95	59	.617	3.0
1919	80	59	.576	7.5
1918	60	63	.488	13.5
1917	71	82	.464	28.5
1916	80	74	.519	11.0
1915	69	83	.454	32.5
1914	70	84	.455	30.0
1913	57	94	.377	38.0
1912	50	102	.329	55.0
1911	76	76	.500	25.5
1910	88	63	.583	14.5
1909	74	77	.490	23.5
1908	51	103	.331	39.5
1907	70	78	.473	21.0
1906	90	61	.596	3.0
1905	71	78	.477	21.5
1904	92	59	.609	1.5
1903	72	62	.537	17.0
1902	50	88	.362	34.0
1901	68	65	.511	13.5

New York Yankees Postseason Results

2006	AL Division Series	Detroit Tigers	Lost, 3—1
2005	AL Division Series	Anaheim Angels	Lost, 3—2
2004	AL Championship Series	Boston Red Sox	Lost, 3—4
	AL Division Series	Minnesota Twins	Won, 3—1
2003	World Series	Florida Marlins	Lost, 4—2
	AL Championship Series	Boston Red Sox	Won, 4—3
	AL Division Series	Minnesota Twins	Won, 3—1
2002	AL Division Series	Anaheim Angels	Lost, 3—1
2001	World Series	Arizona Diamondbacks	Lost, 4—3
	AL Championship Series	Seattle Mariners	Won, 4—1
	AL Division Series	Oakland A's	Won, 3—2
2000	World Series	New York Mets	Won, 4—1
	AL Championship Series	Seattle Mariners	Won, 4—2
	AL Division Series	Oakland A's	Won, 3—2
1999	World Series	Atlanta Braves	Won, 4—0
	Al Championship Series	Boston Red Sox	Won, 4—1
	AL Division Series	Texas Rangers	Won, 3—0
1998	World Series	San Diego Padres	Won, 4—0
	AL Championship Series	Cleveland Indians	Won, 4—2
	AL Division Series	Texas Rangers	Won, 3—0
1997	AL Division Series	Cleveland Indians	Lost, 3—2
1996	World Series	Atlanta Braves	Won, 4—2
	AL Championship Series	Baltimore Orioles	Won, 4—1
	AL Division Series	Texas Rangers	Won, 3—1
1995	AL Division Series	Seattle Mariners	Lost, 3—2

1981	World Series	Los Angeles Dodgers	Lost, 4—2
	AL Championship Series	Oakland A's	Won, 3—0
	Eastern Division Series	Milwaukee Brewers	Won, 3—2
1980	AL Championship Series	Kansas City Royals	Lost, 3—0
1978	World Series	Los Angeles Dodgers	Won, 4—2
	AL Championship Series	Kansas City Royals	Won, 3—1
1977	World Series	Los Angeles Dodgers	Won, 4—2
	AL Championship Series	Kansas City Royals	Won, 3—2
1976	World Series	Cincinnati Reds	Lost, 4—0
	AL Championship Series	Kansas City Royals	Won, 3—2
1964	World Series	St. Louis Cardinals	Lost, 4—3
1963	World Series	Los Angeles Dodgers	Lost, 4—0
1962	World Series	San Francisco Giants	Won, 4—3
1961	World Series	Cincinnati Reds	Won, 4—1
1960	World Series	Pittsburgh Pirates	Lost, 4—3
1958	World Series	Milwaukee Braves	Won, 4—3
1957	World Series	Milwaukee Braves	Lost, 4—3
1956	World Series	Brooklyn Dodgers	Won, 4—3
1955	World Series	Brooklyn Dodgers	Lost, 4—3
1953	World Series	Brooklyn Dodgers	Won, 4—2
1952	World Series	Brooklyn Dodgers	Won, 4—3
1951	World Series	New York Giants	Won, 4—2
1950	World Series	Philadelphia Phillies	Won, 4—0
1949	World Series	Brooklyn Dodgers	Won, 4—1
1947	World Series	Brooklyn Dodgers	Won, 4—3
1943	World Series	St. Louis Cardinals	Won, 4—1
1942	World Series	St. Louis Cardinals	Lost, 4—1

1941	World Series	Brooklyn Dodgers	Won, 4—1
1939	World Series	Cincinnati Reds	Won, 4—0
1938	World Series	Chicago Cubs	Won, 4—0
1937	World Series	New York Giants	Won, 4—1
1936	World Series	New York Giants	Won, 4—2
1932	World Series	Chicago Cubs	Won, 4—0
1928	World Series	St. Louis Cardinals	Won, 4—0
1927	World Series	Pittsburgh Pirates	Won, 4—0
1926	World Series	St. Louis Cardinals	Lost, 4—3
1923	World Series	New York Giants	Won, 4—2
1922	World Series	New York Giants	Lost, 4—0
1921	World Series	Giants	Lost, 5—3

Total:

26 World Series Championships

39 American League Pennants

New York Yankee Hall of Famers

Player	Years with Yankees
Frank Baker	1916–1919, 1921–1922
Yogi Berra	1946–1963
Wade Boggs	1993–1997
Frank Chance	1913–1914
Jack Chesbro	1903–1909
Earle Combs	1924–1935
Stan Coveleski	1928
Bill Dickey	1928–1943, 1946
Joe DiMaggio	1936–1942, 1946–1951
Leo Durocher	1925, 1928–1929
Whitey Ford	1950, 1953–1967
Lou Gehrig	1923–1939
Lefty Gomez	1930–1942
Clark Griffith	1903–1907
Burleigh Grimes	1934
Waite Hoyt	1921–1930
Catfish Hunter	1975–1979
Reggie Jackson	1977–1981
Willie Keeler	1903–1909
Tony Lazzeri	1926–1937
Mickey Mantle	1951–1968
Bill McKechnie	1913
Johnny Mize	1949–1953
Phil Niekro	1984–1985
Herb Pennock	1923–1933

Player	Years with Yankees
Gaylord Perry	1980
Phil Rizzuto	1941–1942, 1946–1956
Red Ruffing	1930–1942, 1945–1946
Babe Ruth	1920–1934
Joe Sewell	1931–1933
Enos Slaughter	1954–1959
Dazzy Vance	1915, 1918
Paul Waner	1944–1945
Dave Winfield	1981–1988, 1990

Matt Christopher®

Sports Bio Bookshelf

Muhammad Ali

Lance Armstrong

Kobe Bryant

Jennifer Capriati

Dale Earnhardt Sr.

Jeff Gordon

Ken Griffey Jr.

Mia Hamm

Tony Hawk

Ichiro

Derek Jeter

Randy Johnson

Michael Jordan

Mario Lemieux

Mark McGwire

Yao Ming

Shaquille O'Neal

Jackie Robinson

Alex Rodriguez

Babe Ruth

Curt Schilling

Sammy Sosa

Venus and Serena
Williams

Tiger Woods

The #1
Sports Series
for Kids

MATT CHRISTOPHER®

Read them all!

*Previously published as Crackerjack Halfback

All available in paperback from Little, Brown and Company

**Previously published as Pressure Play